BIG STITCH
CROSS STITCH

BIG STITCH
CROSS STITCH

Over 30 Contemporary Cross Stitch
Projects Using Extra-Large Stitches

Jacqui Pearce

NORTH LIGHT BOOKS

For my Mom— forever my craft inspiration and support.
And to Gareth, Libby, and Fin—for your love and hugs.
PS: Dora, I hope you approve x

First published in the United Kingdom in 2012 as *Supersize Stitches* by Fil Rouge Press, 1110 Seddon House, London EC2Y 8BX.

Text, project designs and practical illustrations and photography © Jacqui Pearce 2012
Book layout and photographs of finished projects
© Fil Rouge Press Ltd 2012

Manufactured in China.

Published by North Light Books, an imprint of F+W Media, Inc., 10151 Carver Road, Suite 200, Blue Ash, Ohio 45242. (800) 289-0963. First Edition.

fw

F+W PUBLICATIONS, INC.

www.fwmedia.com

SRN: W8770
ISBN-13: 978-1-4403-2138-2

contents

introduction

My childhood in 1970s England was in a home full of color, pattern, and madly bright homespun crafts, influenced by two ladies from the original "Make Do and Mend Generation:" my grandmother, Dora, and my mom. The family's floral-covered Singer sewing machine was used to create matching rick-rack decorated outfits for me and my sister, and it became the machine that I learned how to sew on, took to university, and indeed still have in my studio today. Crafty things were everywhere in my life —my mom earned extra money working part-time in our local craft store, "Patricia's," and her emporium of haberdashery goodies was like treasure to me. It was there that I discovered cross stitch and created some of my earliest "works" on cotton binca. Back in those times many folks stitched, knitted, and sewed their own home crafts, and it seemed to me that over the years these crafts became thought of as tacky or lame, and somehow stuck in a time warp.

Fast forward to a life after a textile degree and a career in the fashion trade to 2005, just after my daughter was born. We went to Palm Springs, California, where I met a whole host of artists working in ceramics and textiles, and they re-ignited my love of homespun crafts. One in particular worked in needlepoint, creating mad, graphic 1970s patterns, and so my passion for yarn on canvas began. The big stitches appealed to my lack of patience, and the bright, wooly finish was simply luscious.

Like all the best passions, what started as a hobby became a business a few years later, when, purely by accident, a trade buyer saw some of my pillows ... and so my professional crafty story began.

This book is an introduction to a new generation of cross stitch designs. Bold, bright, and quick to stitch, the patterns have mainly been created with big count bases and woolen tapestry yarn in mind. However, what I love about this craft is that it is adaptable. Any of the patterns can be used for more traditional needlepoint or cross stitch bases, so if you have a favorite technique or stash, then the choice is yours, though large count canvas and tapestry yarn are my weapons of choice. I hope that I can inspire you to create some of your own supersize stitches.

quick start guide

If you are keen to get going, I have created a quick start guide to stitching. If you know what you are doing, read no further—simply choose your project, check the stitch stats for the required tools and materials, then follow the chart and key, and count your stitches as you work.

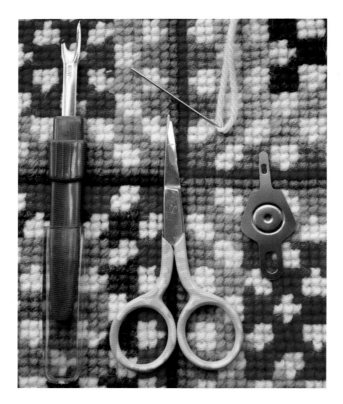

used in embroidery and quilting projects as it is in canvas work. Cross stitch uses two threads that are crossed at right angles and worked over a grid of squares to create a pattern. Each square on the grid is a single stitch. It is normally worked on Aida or evenweave cloths with stitch bases ranging from 6–28 count (holes and therefore stitches per inch).

Needlepoint is defined as woolen yarn worked on open canvas, usually with single diagonal stitches (tent, basket-weave, or half cross stitch), from 3 to 14 count. While you can use my patterns for this method, I have completed all of my designs using simple cross stitch (see page 147)—so basically this book is a hybrid of these two styles. **Wool + canvas + cross stitch = Big Cross Stitch** Why? Because it is my favorite method, and this book is all about showing how you can use supersize cross stitches to create modern quick stitch projects. If you prefer more traditional cross stitch bases I have suggested alternatives with each project, and a conversion chart for the yarns on page 149.

ready steady stitch!

For beginners or folks who want to brush up on their technique I have created a more comprehensive **stitch techniques** section at the back of the book (see page 140). Here you can learn about what you need in your stitch stash, how to stitch, and how to start and finish your projects in more detail.

so is this needlepoint or cross stitch?

There are a plethora of opinions on the matter, of which I will share a few. Cross stitch is a traditional craft steeped in folklore. It had no defined beginning and is as popular

tools and materials

You do not have to invest a fortune to start stitching—base, yarn, a needle, and scissors are all that you need. For this book, I have mainly used 7-count canvas worked with 4-ply tapestry wool, but there are some patterns where I have used alternatives. Each of the following projects gives you a "recipe" detailing the **base, yarn** and a **key** for yarn colors with the amount you will require. There is also a reference to the number of stitches (to give you an idea of how long it may take you), plus the finished size of the piece.

My signature palette is a rainbow of bright colors, so while most manufacturers create more than 400 colors I limit

charts and starting off

I have created colored charts for this book. Each colored square is a complete stitch and the color of the square coordinates with a color on the yarn key. There is a comprehensive guide to **getting started** on pages 145–9. Once you have prepared your base and thread, simply follow the pattern, remembering to keep your wooly stitches going in the same direction (left and right, or up and down). If you don't then the finished texture of the completed tapestry looks "odd."

work in progress

Many books recommend using a tapestry frame to keep your work square. I have never used one of these as the wool is very forgiving at the finishing stage (see page 150), although I do use a 4-in (10-cm) hoop when working on evenweave or Aida.

The best thing about cross stitch as a craft is just how portable it is. You only need a small bag (anything will do) or you can simply pop it in your purse to stitch when you are out. I use a drawstring bag to carry my current projects around (yes, I usually have at least two different things on the go at a time), and I have stitched while traveling on planes and trains, and even in an auto.

my main palette to less than 15. This means that if you are new to this style of cross stitch, it will not cost you a lot of money to create your own stash of wooly yarns. You can buy the various bases by the foot/meter (see **resources** page 158) and there is a more detailed **stitching kit** section on pages 142–4. I would recommend that you cut your base to 2–4 in (5–10 cm) bigger than the finished project size shown.

levels and difficulty

I have taught cross stitch to six-year-old school children. One of the reasons I love this craft so much is that it is super easy to create stunning results. All it takes is a little time to learn the basic method (see pages 145–7) and then you can get going. I have graded each of the projects with a different level (see box, above) to help guide you.

HUGE HOME COMFORTS

I have created projects that will not only bring a dash of stylish color to your home, but also a huge dose of comfort! There are of course LOTS of pillows, still my most popular kits, and I have created simple squares and also some stylish shapes to inspire you. The finished tapestries can equally be used to cover a chair or a stool. And I have even made a pouffe!

XXL pillow trio

This trio of plump pillows is a homage to retro computer keyboards. The giant font and the combination of letters that stand for extra, extra large sum up my take on huge home style.

method

1 Prepare your base and find the middle by folding in half and half again.

2 Following the yarn keys on pages 14 and 16, find the color shown for the letter you are stitching.

3 Thread your needle using a single strand of the yarn.

4 Begin to stitch from the middle of the canvas—working left to right, following the chart.

5 Stitch the letter first, continuing to stitch left to right along the rows. Then work your way outward to complete the canvas, filling in the outer color last.

tools and materials

- 7-count canvas, 20 x 20 in (50 x 50 cm), for each pillow
- 4-ply Appleton Tapestry Yarn—see thread key on page 14
- Size 18 tapestry needle
- Threader (optional)
- Backing fabric, 20 x 27½ in (50 x 70 cm), for each pillow
- Matching sewing thread
- Pillow pad, 16 in (40 cm) square
- Rainbow trim (optional)
- Sewing machine to make up

thread key

FINISHED MOTIF SIZE: 14½ in (37 cm) w
X 14½ in (37 cm) h

Color	Hanks	Type	Number	Name
	1.5	Appleton	992	Ivory
■	1	Appleton	993	Black
■	1.5	Appleton	486	Kingfisher

thread key

FINISHED MOTIF SIZE: 14½ in (37 cm) w
X 14½ in (37 cm) h

Color	Hanks	Type	Number	Name
	1.5	Appleton	992	Ivory
■	1	Appleton	993	Black
■	1.5	Appleton	253	Grass Green

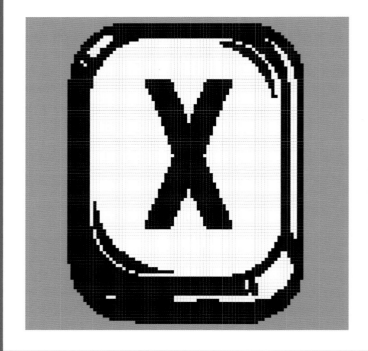

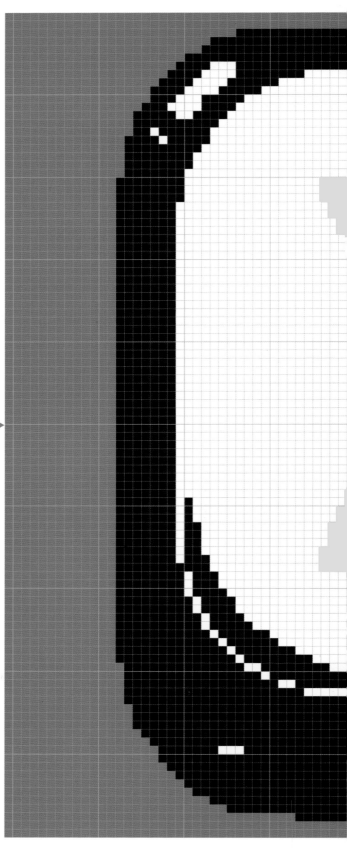

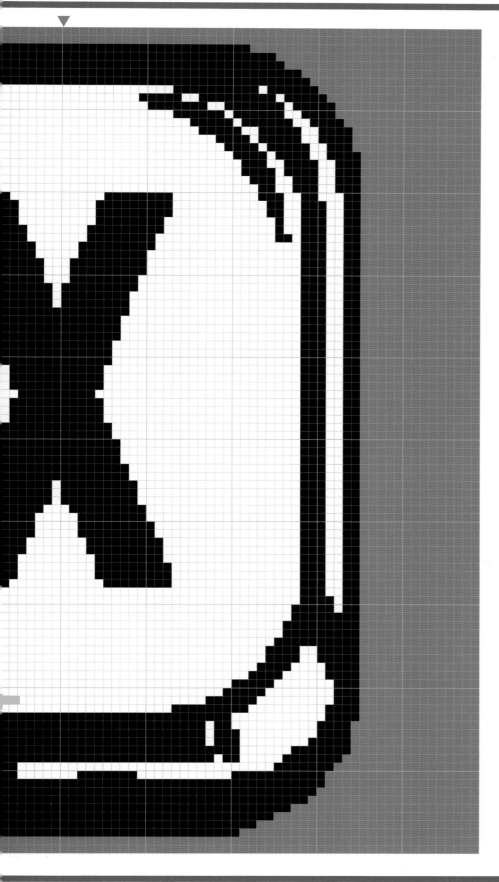

variations

● You could change the letter in the middle of your pillow—just see how many squares you have in the middle of the chart and using a piece of graph or squared paper color in your shape to stitch.

finishing

1 Block/press your finished tapestry, following the directions on page 150.

2 Trim the tapestry edges to leave a 1-in (2.5-cm) seam allowance around the edge of your work.

3 Follow the directions on pages 153 and 155–6 for making up a regular envelope back pillow and adding your chosen trim.

4 Put in your pillow pad to complete your huge home-style project.

5 Follow the directions on pages 12–16 for each individual pillow.

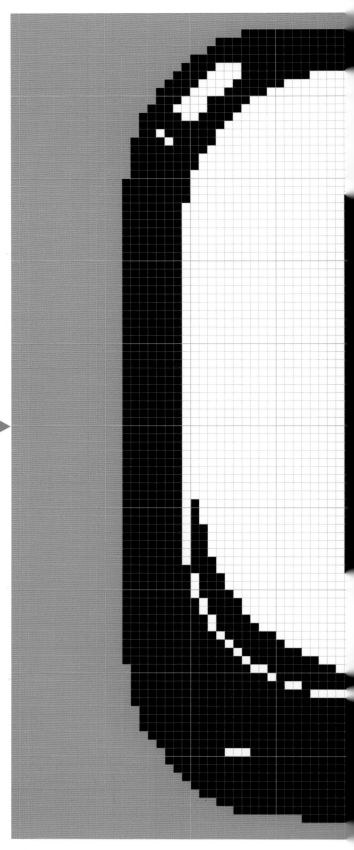

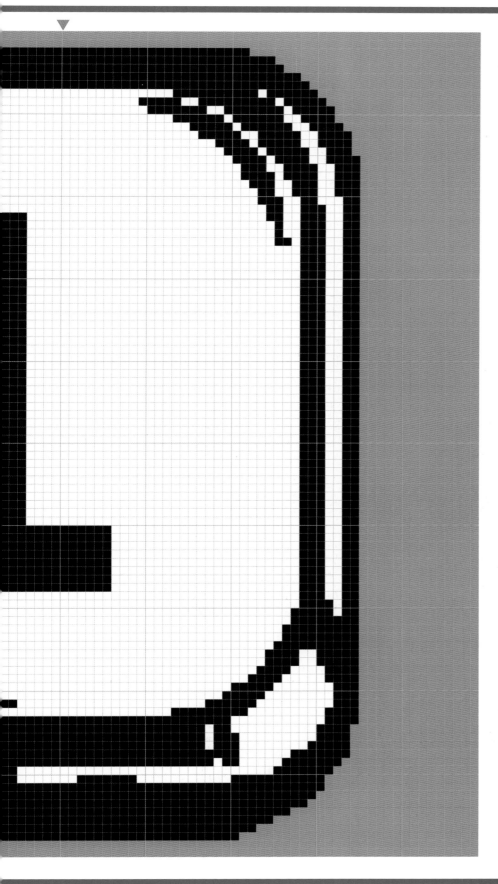

variations

● Refer to the chart on page 149 for yarn conversion to other tapestry yarn colors.

2 heart swirl pillow

This swirly love heart pillow is a perfect display of affection—
I love how the pinks and reds swirl together like retro candy. It will
look equally delicious on your couch as in your boudoir.

stitch stats

stitches: 84 x 81 shaped
yarn: Appleton tapestry wool
base: 5-count canvas
skill level: 2

tools and materials

- 5-count canvas, 21½ x 21½ in (55 x 55 cm), you can trim this later
- 4-ply Appleton Tapestry Yarn—see thread key on page 20
- Size 14 tapestry needle
- Threader (optional)
- Backing fabric, 21½ x 21½ in (55 x 55 cm)
- Matching sewing thread
- Heart-shaped pillow pad or filling and canvas to make your own
- Sewing machine to make up

method

1 Prepare your base and find the middle by folding in half and half again.

2 Following the yarn key on page 20 find your starting color for the middle.

3 Thread your needle using two strands of the 4-ply tapestry yarn.

4 Begin to stitch from the middle of the canvas—working left to right, following the chart.

5 Complete the middle heart first and then work outward one swirl at a time.

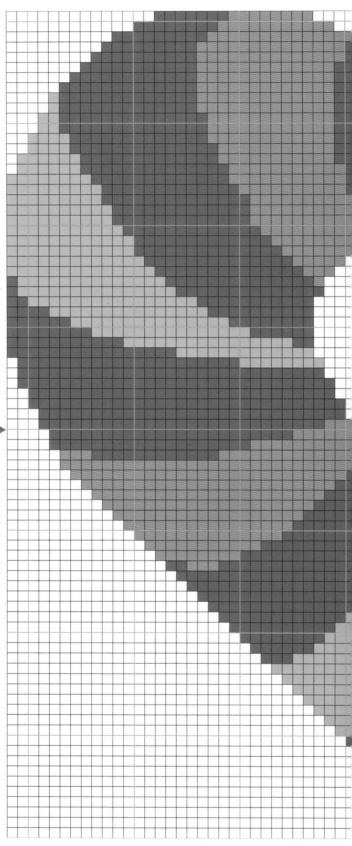

thread key

FINISHED MOTIF SIZE: 17 in (43 cm) w
X 16 in (41 cm) h

Color	Hanks	Type	Number	Name
	0.75	Appleton	992	Ivory
	2	Appleton	995	Red
	1	Appleton	943	Pink
	1	Appleton	945	Dark Pink

finishing

1 Block/press your finished tapestry, following the directions on page 150.

2 Trim the tapestry edges to leave a 1-in (2.5-cm) seam allowance around the edge of your work.

3 Follow the directions on page 153 for making up a template pattern for your backing fabric.

4 Follow the directions on pages 155–6 for making up a pillow.

variations

● Refer to the chart on page 149 for yarn conversion to other tapestry yarn colors.

3 granny square pillow

I am a keen crochet fan—and cherish the granny square blankets my mom made. I decided that it would be interesting to turn this classic pattern into cross stitch and I am thrilled with the result.

stitch stats

stitches: 120 x 120
yarn: Appleton tapestry wool
base: 7-count canvas
skill level: 2

tools and materials

- 7-count canvas, 21½ x 21½ in (55 x 55 cm), you can trim this later
- 4-ply Appleton Tapestry Yarn—see thread key on page 24
- Size 18 tapestry needle
- Threader (optional)
- Backing fabric, 21½ x 29½ in (55 x 75 cm)
- Matching sewing thread
- Sewing machine to make up
- Pillow pad, 17¾ in (45 cm) square
- Trim (optional)

method

1 Prepare your base and find the middle by folding in half and half again.

2 Following the yarn key on page 24, find the color shown in the middle.

3 Thread your needle using a single strand of the yarn and begin to stitch from the middle of the canvas—working left to right, following the chart.

4 Complete the middle of the flower first and work outward to complete the middle piece.

5 Then stitch a color at a time, working out from the middle, continuing to stitch left to right along the rows.

6 Work your way outward to complete the canvas and border, then finally fill in the ivory bits in between.

thread key

FINISHED MOTIF SIZE: 17 in (43 cm) w

X 17 in (43 cm) h

Color	Hanks	Type	Number	Name
	2	Appleton	992	Ivory
	0.5	Appleton	995	Red
	0.25	Appleton	445	Orange
	0.5	Appleton	553	Yellow
	0.5	Appleton	253	Grass Green
	0.5	Appleton	481	Turquoise
	0.5	Appleton	486	Kingfisher
	0.5	Appleton	943	Pink
	0.5	Appleton	945	Dark Pink
	0.5	Appleton	456	Purple

finishing

1 Block/press your finished tapestry, following the directions on page 150.

2 Trim the tapestry edges to leave a 1-in (2.5-cm) seam allowance around the edge of your work.

3 Follow the directions on pages 155–6 for making up a regular envelope-back style pillow, and also method choices for adding the trim.

4 Put in your pillow pad to complete your pillow. It's ready to admire!

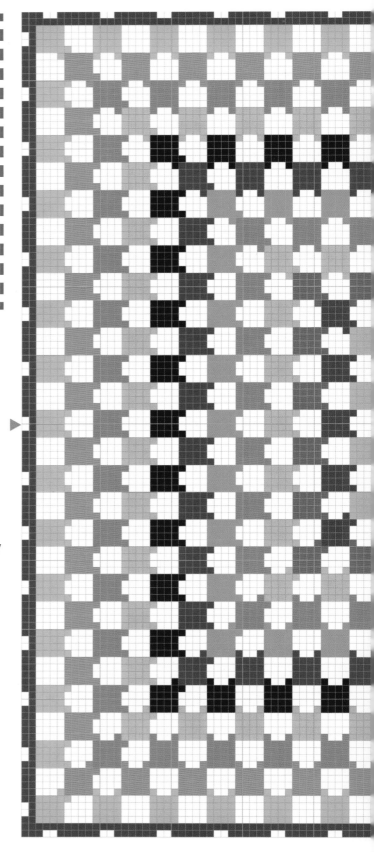

variations

● Refer to the chart on page 149 for yarn conversion to other tapestry yarn colors.

● I think this would make a fantastic rug—and you could stitch on 5 HPI canvas, or simply keep repeating the pattern out on the 7 count (as you would if you were crocheting).

4 groovy circles pillow

This project was inspired by the psychedelic graphics of my mom's collection of 1970s vinyl covers. The design's simplicity mixed with the bold colors make this a groovy project to stitch.

tools and materials

- 7-count canvas, 16 x 16 in (40 x 40 cm)
- 4-ply Appleton Tapestry Yarn—see thread key on page 28
- Size 18 tapestry needle
- Threader (optional)
- Backing fabric, 16 x 23 in (40 x 60 cm)
- Matching sewing thread
- Sewing machine to make up
- Pillow pad, 14 in (35 cm) square
- Trim (optional)

method

1 Prepare your base and find the middle by folding in half and half again.

2 Following the yarn key on page 28, find the color shown in the middle.

3 Thread your needle using a single strand of the yarn and begin to stitch from the middle of the canvas, working left to right, following the chart.

4 Complete the middle first and work outward to complete the central diamond.

5 Then stitch a color at a time, working out from the middle, continuing to stitch left to right along the rows.

6 Work your way outward to complete the colored motif, then fill in the ivory background.

thread key

FINISHED MOTIF SIZE: 12 in (30 cm) w
X 12 in (30 cm) h

Color	Hanks	Type	Number	Name
	0.5	Appleton	992	Ivory
	0.5	Appleton	995	Red
	0.25	Appleton	474	Golden Yellow
	0.25	Appleton	253	Grass Green
	0.25	Appleton	481	Turquoise
	0.75	Appleton	489	Dark Kingfisher
	0.1	Appleton	943	Pink

finishing

1 Block/press your finished tapestry, following the directions on page 150.

2 Trim the tapestry edges to leave a 1-in (2.5-cm) seam allowance around the edge of your work.

3 Follow the directions on pages 155–6 for making up a regular envelope-back style pillow, and also method choices for adding the trim.

4 Put in your pillow pad to complete your pillow. It's ready to admire!

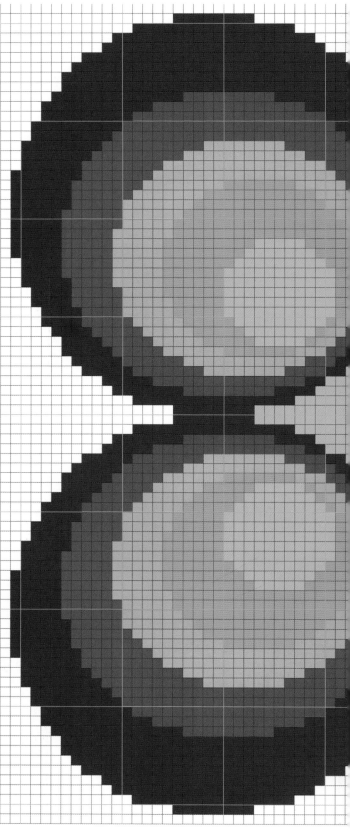

variations

● Refer to the chart on page 149 for yarn conversion to other tapestry yarn colors.

5 bright bloom tile pillow

My grandma had a collection of enamel pans decorated with a colorful floral pattern that I adored as a child. Inspired by these mad kitchen graphics I have created a bloom for all seasons.

stitch stats

stitches: 135 x 135
yarn: Appleton tapestry wool
base: 7-count canvas
skill level: 2

method

1 Prepare your base and find the middle by folding in half and half again.

2 Following the yarn key on page 32, find the color shown in the middle.

3 Thread your needle using a single strand of the yarn and begin to stitch from the middle of the canvas—working left to right, following the chart to complete the X pattern in the middle first.

4 Work outward, finishing the middle motif and then one by one the rainbow nuggets, color by color.

5 Continue stitching left to right along the rows—working the flowers and then outer border.

6 Work your way outward to complete the canvas and fill in the ivory background last.

tools and materials

- 7-count canvas, 23 x 23 in (60 x 60 cm)
- 4-ply Appleton Tapestry Yarn—see thread key on page 32
- Size 18 tapestry needle
- Threader (optional)
- Backing fabric, 20 x 27½ in (50 x 70 cm)
- Matching sewing thread
- Sewing machine to make up
- Pillow pad, 16 in (40 cm) square
- Trim (optional)

thread key

FINISHED MOTIF SIZE: 20 in (50 cm) w
X 20 in (50 cm) h

Color	Hanks	Type	Number	Name
	2.5	Appleton	992	Ivory
	0.5	Appleton	995	Red
	0.5	Appleton	445	Orange
	0.25	Appleton	474	Golden Yellow
	0.5	Appleton	253	Grass Green
	1	Appleton	481	Turquoise
	0.25	Appleton	456	Purple
	1.25	Appleton	943	Pink

finishing

1 Block/press your finished tapestry, following the directions on page 150.

2 Trim the tapestry edges to leave a 1-in (2.5-cm) seam allowance around the edge of your work.

3 Follow the directions on pages 155–6 for making up a regular envelope-back style pillow, and also method choices for adding the trim.

4 Put in your pillow pad to complete your pillow. It's ready to admire!

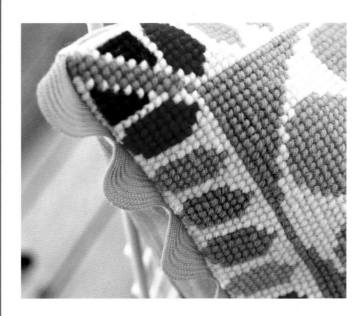

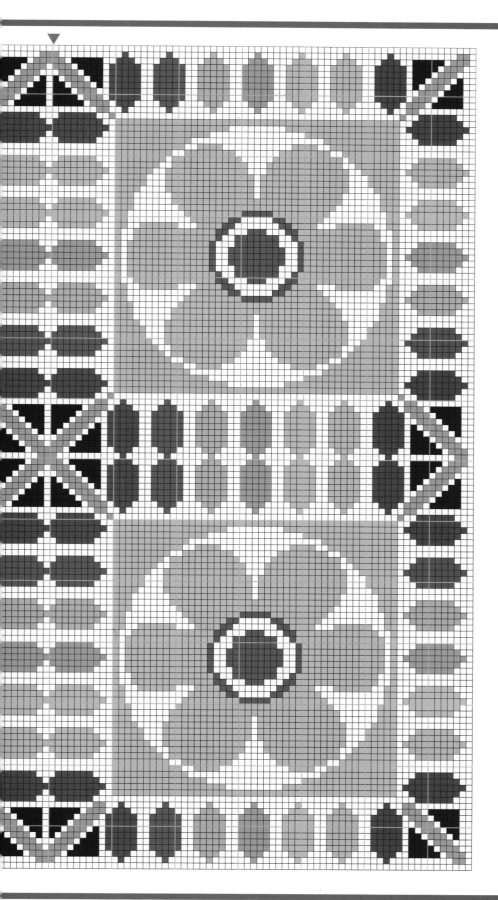

variations

● Refer to the chart on page 149 for yarn conversion to other tapestry yarn colors.

● I have made a matching picture in 5 count (see page 106), which you may like to stitch to complete the look. You can always stitch the picture in matching 7 count if you prefer—just bear in mind that it will be smaller.

6 russian doll pillow

Russian dolls have a charm that has inspired designers over the years. This supersize shaped doll sits well in a child's bedroom, but is equally at home on a couch ... you could make it in staggered sizes!

tools and materials

- 5-count canvas, 20 x 23 in (50 x 60 cm), you can trim this later
- 4-ply Appleton Tapestry Yarn—see thread key on page 36
- Size 14 tapestry needle
- Threader (optional)
- Backing fabric, 20 x 23 in (50 x 60 cm)
- Matching sewing thread
- Sewing machine to make up
- Pillow filler

stitch stats
stitches: 71 x 91
yarn: Appleton tapestry wool
base: 5-count canvas
skill level: 2

method

1 Prepare your base and find the middle by folding in half and half again.

2 Following the yarn key on page 36, choose the hood color.

3 Thread your needle using two strands of the 4-ply tapestry yarn.

4 Count the stitch holes up from the middle of the canvas and begin to stitch the hood from the middle of the canvas—working left to right, following the chart.

5 Complete the hood, then the hair, and finally the face.

6 Move onto the ribbon trim detail and work your way outward and downward until you have completed the canvas.

variations

● Refer to the chart on page 149 for yarn conversion to other tapestry yarn colors.

● I think it would be great fun to make a few of these Russian dolls in different sizes. All you need to do is stitch up the same chart but use higher count base fabrics (which will make them smaller).

● A 7-count canvas doll will measure 10 x 13 in/25 x 33 cm (stitch with one thread of tapestry yarn).

● A 10-count canvas doll will measure 7 x 9 in/18 x 23 cm (stitch with two threads of crewel yarn).

thread key

FINISHED MOTIF SIZE: 14¼ in (36 cm) w
X 18 in (46 cm) h

Color	Hanks	Type	Number	Name
	0.5	Appleton	992	Ivory
	1	Appleton	995	Red
	0.25	Appleton	445	Orange
	0.25	Appleton	474	Golden Yellow
	0.25	Appleton	253	Grass Green
	1	Appleton	481	Turquoise
	1	Appleton	486	Kingfisher
	0.5	Appleton	943	Pink
	0.5	Appleton	456	Purple
	0.5	Appleton	993	Black

finishing

1 Block/press your finished tapestry, following the directions on page 150.

2 Trim the tapestry edges to leave a 1-in (2.5-cm) seam allowance around the edge of your work.

3 Follow the directions on pages 152–3 for making up a template pattern for your backing fabric.

4 Follow the directions on pages 155–6 for making up a pillow.

7 groovy pouffe

I love the colorful Moroccan leather pouffes and slippers that you find in stylish home stores. So in this project I have gone all-out on the color to make a thoroughly modern pouffe.

stitch stats

stitches: 148 diameter
yarn: Appleton tapestry wool
base: 7-count canvas
skill level: 3

method

1 Prepare your base and find the middle by folding in half and half again.

2 Following the yarn key on page 40, choose the middle color.

3 Thread your needle using a single strand of the 4-ply tapestry yarn.

4 Work outward from the middle a color section at a time, making sure that you are stitching in the same direction.

5 Work all the detail elements first, then fill in the blue and purple backgrounds last.

tools and materials

- 7-count canvas, 27½ x 27½ in (70 x 70 cm, you can trim this later)
- 4-ply Appleton Tapestry Yarn—see thread key on page 40
- Size 18 tapestry needle
- Threader (optional)
- 23-in (60-cm) square piece of fabric for base, 16 x 65-in (40 x 165-cm) piece for side (or 2 pieces, 16 x 33 in/40 x 85 cm, sewn together)
- Matching sewing thread
- Sewing machine to make up
- Shirts/sheets, towels or LOTs of pillow filling

thread key

FINISHED MOTIF SIZE: 21¼ in (54 cm) diameter

Color	Hanks	Type	Number	Name
	0.25	Appleton	992	Ivory
	0.5	Appleton	995	Red
	0.25	Appleton	445	Orange
	0.25	Appleton	474	Golden Yellow
	0.1	Appleton	253	Grass Green
	2	Appleton	481	Turquoise
	0.5	Appleton	486	Kingfisher
	0.5	Appleton	943	Pink
	2	Appleton	456	Purple

finishing

1 Block/press your finished tapestry, following the directions on page 150.

2 Trim the tapestry edges to leave a 1-in (2.5-cm) seam allowance around the edge of your work.

3 Follow the directions on pages 152–3 for making up a template pattern for your edge and base.

4 Follow the directions on page 157 for making up your pouffe.

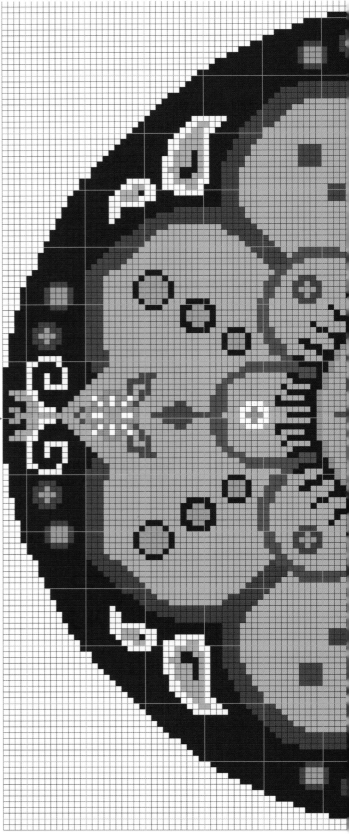

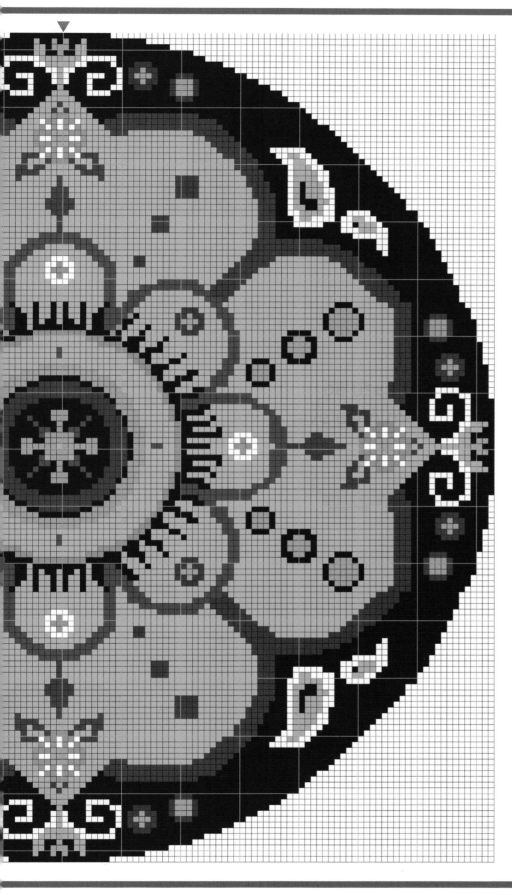

variations

- Refer to the chart on page 149 for yarn conversion to other tapestry yarn colors.

top tip

- I used lots of old sheets and my husband's shirts to stuff my pouffe, finishing off with plenty of old scraps of fabric. It takes lots of fabric to stuff, but it gives a real weight to your finished piece, and means that it will not collapse when someone sits on it. It also is quite forgiving when reshaping after use.

rainbow cozy

A pot of tea on a Sunday morning with the newspapers is a tradition in our house, and this rainbow tea cozy will bring a little sunshine to any teapot or place setting.

stitch stats

stitches: 86 x 65 shaped top
yarn: Appleton tapestry wool
base: 7-count canvas
skill level: 2

method

1 Prepare your base and find the middle by folding in half and half again.

2 Following the yarn key on page 44, choose the cloud edge color.

3 Thread your needle using a single strand of the 4-ply tapestry yarn.

4 Count the stitch holes up from the middle of the canvas and begin to stitch the outside of the cloud, trying to keep your stitches in the same direction.

5 Complete the cloud and raindrops, then start on the rainbow.

6 Working from the top down, follow the chart a color at a time.

7 Fill in the blue color at the end when all the other colors are done.

tools and materials

- 7-count canvas, 16 x 14 in (40 x 35 cm), you can trim this later
- 4-ply Appleton Tapestry Yarn—see thread key on page 44
- Size 18 tapestry needle
- Threader (optional)
- Backing fabric, 16 x 14 in (40 x 35 cm)
- Lining fabric, 2 x 16 x 14 in (40 x 35 cm)
- Wadding, 2 x 16 x 14 in (40 x 35 cm)
- Matching sewing thread
- Sewing machine to make up
- Pom-pom for top (optional)

thread key

FINISHED MOTIF SIZE: 12 in (30 cm) w
X 9½ in (24 cm) h

Color	Hanks	Type	Number	Name
	0.5	Appleton	992	Ivory
	0.25	Appleton	963	Gray
	0.25	Appleton	995	Red
	0.25	Appleton	445	Orange
	0.25	Appleton	553	Yellow
	0.25	Appleton	253	Grass Green
	0.5	Appleton	481	Turquoise
	0.25	Appleton	945	Dark Pink

finishing

1 Block/press your finished tapestry, following the directions on page 150.

2 Trim the tapestry edges to leave a 1-in (2.5-cm) seam allowance around the edge of your work.

3 Follow the directions on page 153 for making up and using a template pattern for your backing fabrics.

4 Follow the directions on page 156 for making up a tea cozy and page 157 for making a pom-pom.

variations

● Refer to the chart on page 149 for yarn conversion to other tapestry yarn colors.

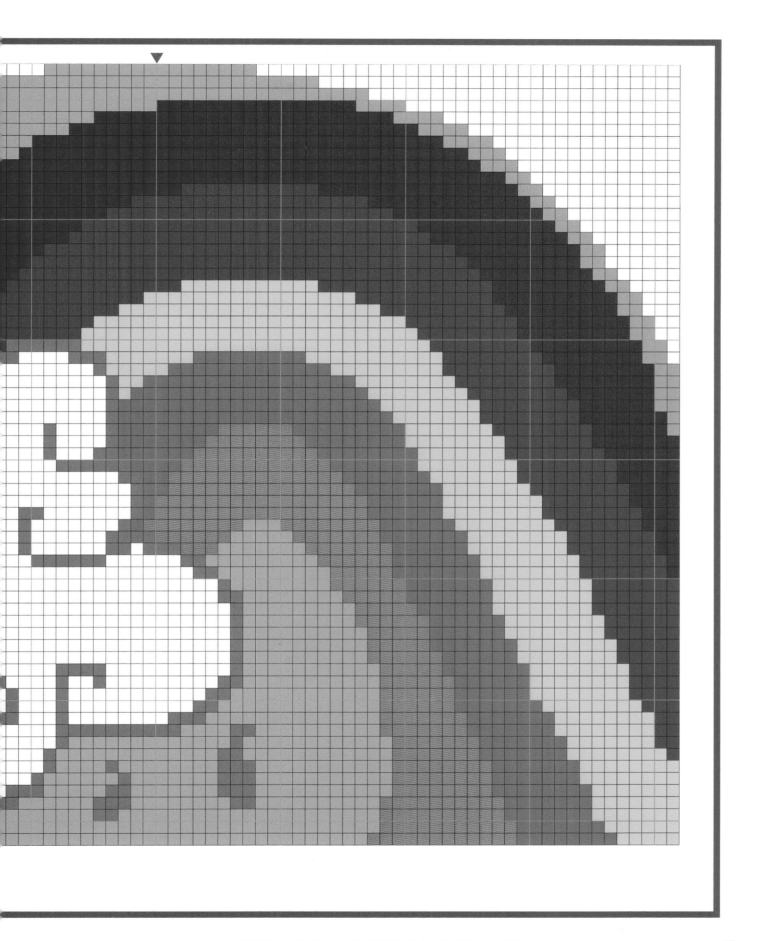

GIGANTIC GIFTS

Whether the gift is for a child or on the day of a wedding, there is nothing so special as a handmade present. The gesture is all the more delightful knowing that it is something created or embellished by your own fair hands! This chapter is all about giving and I have created some quick-stitch presents to wow your very favorite people, as well as some heritage pieces to cherish for a lifetime. From mini badges to groovy cases, there is something for all—and remember you can always treat yourself!

9 crayon pencil case

Colorful crayons are synonymous with childrens' desks and coloring activities. This case for pencils or crayons makes a lovely mini gift or even a project to inspire them to start stitching.

tools and materials

- 7-count canvas, 12 x 10in (30 x 25 cm)
- 4-ply Appleton Tapestry Yarn—see thread key on page 50
- Size 18 tapestry needle
- Threader (optional)
- Lining fabric, 2 x 12 x 25 in (30 x 25 cm)
- Backing fabric, 12 x 25 in (30 x 25 cm)
- Plastic tooth zipper, 8½ in (22 cm)
- Matching sewing thread
- Sewing machine to make up

stitch stats

stitches: 58 x 36
yarn: Appleton tapestry wool
base: 7-count canvas
skill level: 1

method

1 Prepare your base. As this is a small piece you can start stitching from the edge and complete one crayon at a time.

2 Following the yarn key on page 50, find the color and thread your needle using a single strand of the yarn.

3 Starting in the bottom right-hand corner, measure in 1 in (2.5 cm) from each edge (approximately 8 holes).

4 Start to stitch the green crayon—left to right. Continue stitching all the crayon colors in the same way (one color at a time is best).

5 When you have finished the crayons you can fill in the black lines and then fill in the background color at the top.

thread key

FINISHED MOTIF SIZE: 8 in (20 cm) w
X 5 in (12 cm) h

Color	Hanks	Type	Number	Name
■	0.25	Appleton	993	Black
□	0.25	Appleton	992	Ivory
■	0.25	Appleton	474	Golden Yellow
■	0.25	Appleton	553	Yellow
■	0.25	Appleton	993	Dark Orange
■	0.25	Appleton	445	Orange
■	0.25	Appleton	945	Dark Pink
■	0.25	Appleton	943	Pink
■	0.25	Appleton	505	Dark Red
■	0.25	Appleton	995	Red
■	0.25	Appleton	456	Purple
■	0.25	Appleton	885	Lilac
■	0.25	Appleton	489	Dark Kingfisher
■	0.25	Appleton	486	Kingfisher
■	0.25	Appleton	483	Dark Turquoise
■	0.25	Appleton	481	Turquoise
■	0.25	Appleton	546	Dark Green
■	0.25	Appleton	253	Grass Green

finishing

1 Block/press your finished tapestry, following the directions on page 150.

2 Trim the tapestry edges to leave a 1-in (2.5-cm) seam allowance around the edge of your work.

3 Follow the directions on page 157 for making up the pencil case.

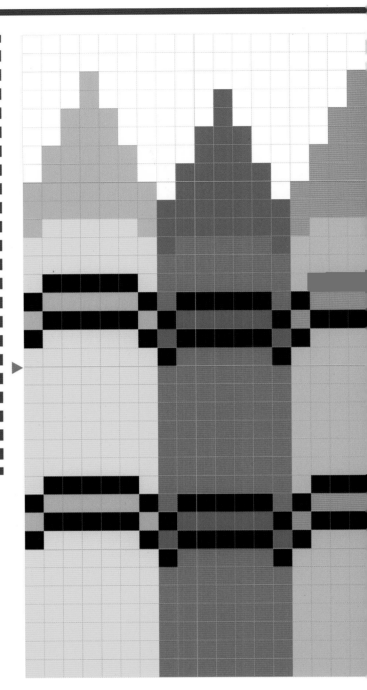

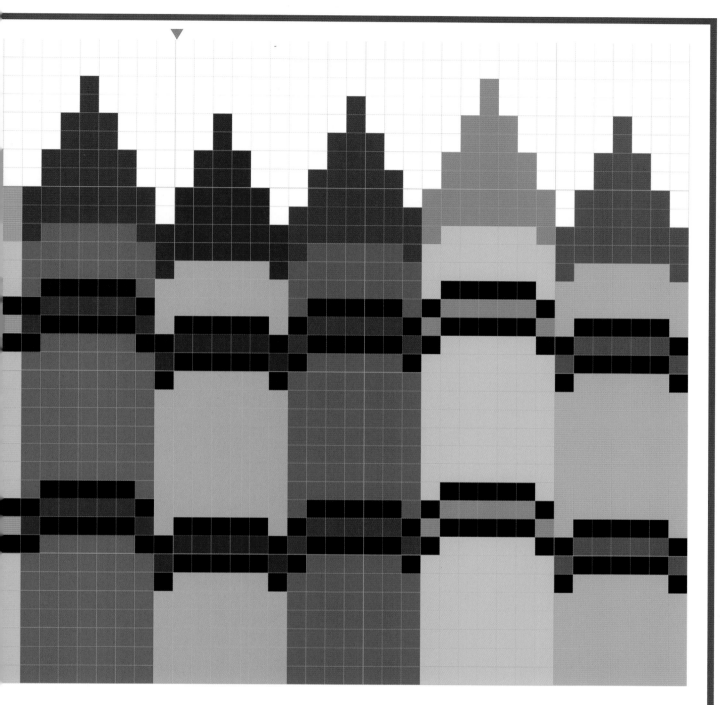

variations

● Refer to the chart on page 149 for yarn conversion to other tapestry yarn colors.

● This also makes a lovely little picture—or you can use it to cover the front of a notebook.

10 boy and girl pillow

I love icons that transcend language and this motif is a classic example. I have added a contemporary graphic pattern to create a pillow which makes a great wedding gift or addition to any home.

tools and materials

- 7-count canvas, 23 x 23 in (60 x 60 cm)
- 4-ply Appleton Tapestry Yarn—see thread key on page 54
- Size 18 tapestry needle
- Threader (optional)
- Backing fabric, 23 x 31 in (60 x 80 cm)
- Matching sewing thread
- Pillow pad, 20 in (50 cm) square
- Trim (optional)
- Sewing machine to make up

method

1 Prepare your base and find the middle by folding in half and half again.

2 Following the yarn key on page 54, find the color shown for the blue diagonal stripe which starts in the middle.

3 Thread your needle using a single strand of the yarn.

4 Begin to stitch from the middle of the canvas, working left to right, following the chart, and completing the first section of diagonal.

5 You can then continue with the diagonals, or switch colors and start to stitch the man.

6 Complete the male half, then switch to the female half and fill in the ivory last.

thread key

FINISHED MOTIF SIZE: 17¾ in (45 cm) w
X 17¾ in (45 cm) h

Color	Hanks	Type	Number	Name
	2	Appleton	992	Ivory
	2	Appleton	995	Red
	2	Appleton	943	Pink
	2	Appleton	481	Turquoise
	2	Appleton	489	Dark Kingfisher

finishing

1 Block/press your finished tapestry, following the directions on page 150.

2 Trim the tapestry edges to leave a 1-in (2.5-cm) seam allowance around the edge of your work.

3 Follow the directions on pages 155–6 for making up a regular envelope back pillow and applying trim.

4 Put in your pillow pad to complete your project. It's ready to admire!

variations

● Refer to the chart on page 149 for yarn conversion to other tapestry yarn colors.

● You could change the pattern to be a repeat of the female side or a repeat of the male side—great if you want to use these in your childrens' rooms or if they are for an individual.

11 bling bling jewel wrap

My grandma used to have an old French silk jewelry roll that she kept her rings in. It was a gift from a friend on her travels. This is my modern interpretation with bling thrown in for good measure.

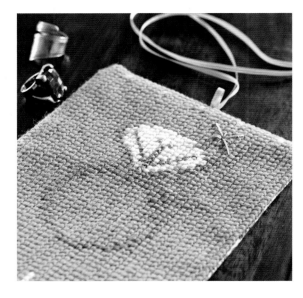

method

1 Prepare your base and find the middle by folding in half and half again.

2 Following the yarn key on page 59, find the color shown for the outside of the ring.

3 Thread your needle using a single strand of the yarn and begin to stitch from the middle of the canvas, working up and down, following the chart to complete the ring, and trying to keep your stitches in the same direction.

4 Complete the ring (leaving gaps for the metallic color), then the stripes and border. Finally, fill in the pink.

5 Last of all, thread your needle with a full strand of the the metallic thread, and fill in the middle of the ring, then work a double cross stitch (see page 148) to add BLING to your ring.

tools and materials

- 7-count canvas, 10 x 16 in (25 x 40 cm)
- 4-ply Appleton Tapestry Yarn—see thread key on page 59
- Size 18 tapestry needle
- Threader (optional)
- Lining fabric, 10 x 16 in (25 x 40 cm), ring holder 4¾ x 16 in (12 x 40 cm)
- Snap fastener
- Ribbon for tying, 20 x ¼-in (50 cm x 5-mm)
- Matching sewing thread
- Sewing machine to make up

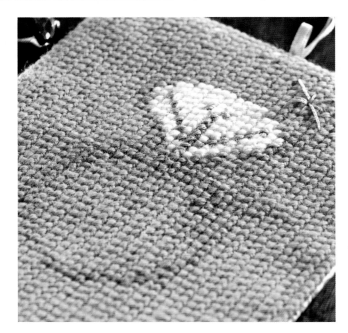

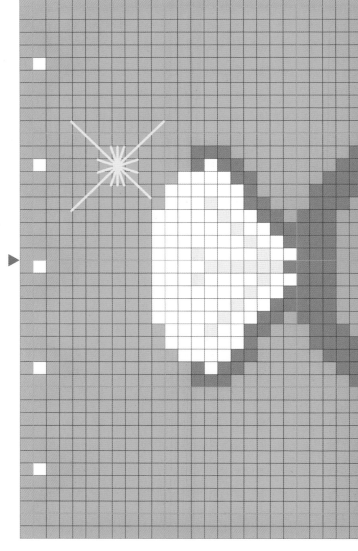

finishing

1 Block/press your finished tapestry, following the instructions on page 150.

2 Trim the tapestry edges to leave a 1-in (2.5-cm) seam allowance around the edge of your work.

3 Cut one lining fabric using the template method on pages 152–3, then cut out a piece for the ring holder 4³⁄₄ x 16 in (12 x 40 cm).

4 Fold the ring holder section in half lengthways (right sides together) to make a tube. Sew along the edge (¹⁄₂-in/1-cm margin), leaving the top and bottom open.

5 Turn the ring holder the right way around. This is fiddly—I find if you attach a safety pin to one open edge and thread the pin back through the tube it makes the process easier.

6 Press, then fold in ¹⁄₂ in (1 cm) at one end of the holder; slip stitch closed, then stitch one side of the snap fastener (giver) to one side of the holder, centered ¹⁄₂ in (1 cm) from the top edge.

7 Measure 1¹⁄₂ in (4 cm) from the middle of the top edge of the right side of the lining fabric and stitch on the other half of the fastener (the receiver).

8 Lightly fill the ring holder with kapok, cotton or scrap yarns, leaving 1¹⁄₄ in (3 cm) free at the other end.

9 Fold under the raw edge of the free end. Stitch this flat section to the lining opposite the snap fastener (receiver) and ¹⁄₂ in (1 cm) in from the edge, making sure that it is centralized and straight.

10 Fold ribbon in half and fold over loop end by ³⁄₄ in (2 cm). Baste to ring end seam allowance at tapestry top (so that loop and 2 ribbon ends hang down work).

11 Place the right sides of lining and tapestry together and sew all the way around, following the edge of the tapestry and leaving a 4-in (10-cm) gap on one side.

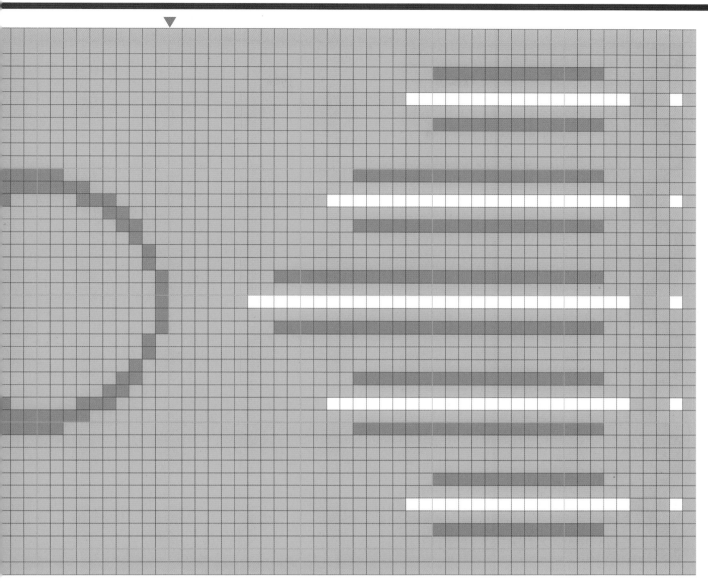

12 Snip the corners, turn the right way around, and press. Slip stitch the opening closed.

13 Simply unstud the ring holder and thread on your rings and pretty things... then fasten, roll up and tie the ribbon around your roll. Secure in the loop with a bow.

variations

● Refer to the chart on page 149 for yarn conversion to other tapestry yarn colors.

● You could make this pattern into a mini pouch or zipper-top purse instead by folding in half and simply lining.

● Follow the instructions on page 156 for a pouch and 157 for a zippered top.

thread key

FINISHED MOTIF SIZE: 6½ in (16 cm) w X 12 in (30 cm) h

Color	Hanks	Type	Number	Name
	0.1	Appleton	992	Ivory
	0.25	Appleton	481	Turquoise
	1	Appleton	943	Pink
	0.25	Appleton	963	Gray
	—	DMC	E168	Metallic Silver

12 groovy granny eyeglass case

My grandma had a pair of what I call "Dame Edna" glasses, which fashionable these days—I have a pair of bright red ones. What better place to keep your glasses than in this super groovy case?

stitch stats

stitches: 62 x 26
yarn: Appleton tapestry wool
base: 7-count canvas
skill level: 1

method

1 Prepare your base and find the middle by folding in half and half again.

2 Following the yarn key on page 62, find the color shown for the glasses.

3 Thread your needle using a single strand of the yarn.

4 Begin to stitch from the middle of the canvas, working the glasses first, and trying to keep your stitching in the same direction.

5 Once the glasses are complete you can start to stitch the zigzag rows, one color at a time until complete.

tools and materials

- 7-count canvas, 14 x 8 in (35 x 20 cm)
- 4-ply Appleton Tapestry Yarn—see thread key on page 62
- Size 18 tapestry needle
- Threader (optional)
- Backing fabric, 14 x 8 in (35 x 20 cm)
- Lining fabric, 2 x 14 x 8 in (35 x 20 cm)
- Matching sewing thread
- Sewing machine to make up

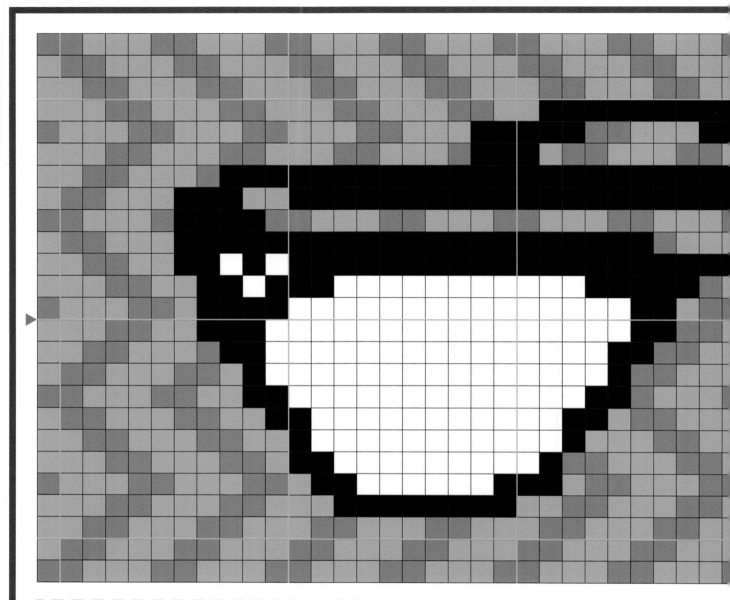

finishing

1 Block/press your finished tapestry, following the directions on page 150.

2 Trim the tapestry edges to leave a 1-in (2.5-cm) seam allowance around the edge of your work.

3 Follow the directions on page 156 for making up a pouch.

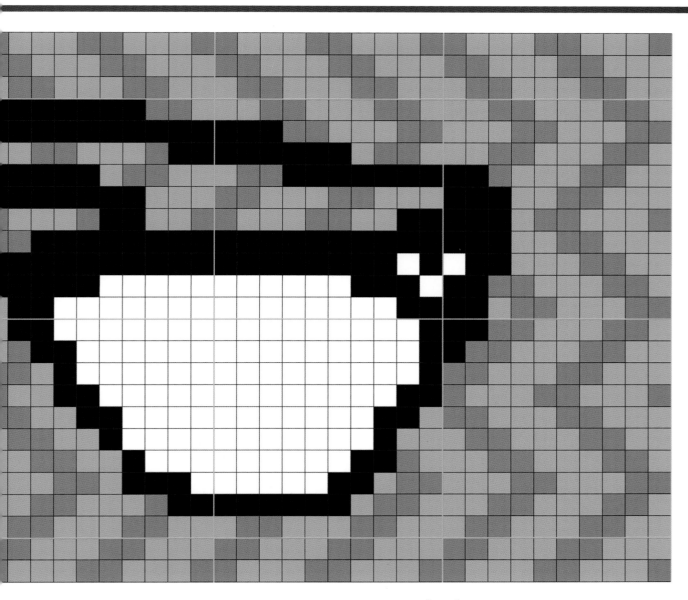

variations

● Refer to the chart on page 149 for yarn conversion to other tapestry yarn colors.

● If your glasses are wider or longer, you can repeat the pattern in the direction required.

● If you do not feel confident repeating the pattern, simply stitch rows of a single color either side to widen or lengthen your pattern. This would look great in a contrasting color—or in black.

● You could even change the color of the glasses to match the color of your own glasses.

13 mix tape tablet cover

My walkman was one of the treasures of my teenage years and I still value this iconic item today. In this digital age I thought I could marry the two with this tablet mix tape cover in rainbow colors.

stitch stats

stitches: 62 x 81
yarn: Appleton tapestry wool
base: 7-count canvas
skill level: 2

tools and materials

- 7-count canvas, 14 x 16 in (35 x 40 cm)
- 4-ply Appleton Tapestry Yarn—see thread key on page 66
- Size 18 tapestry needle
- Threader (optional)
- Backing fabric, 14 x 16 in (35 x 40 cm)
- Lining fabric, 14 x 16 in (35 x 40 cm)
- Matching sewing thread
- Sewing machine to make up

method

1 Prepare your base and find the middle by folding in half and half again.

2 Following the yarn key on page 66, find the color shown for the mix tape outline.

3 Thread your needle using a single strand of the yarn.

4 Begin to stitch from the middle of the canvas, working the outline of the tape and then the tangled tape.

5 I found that it is best to work up and down, following the chart, as it is easier to stitch the rainbow rows.

6 Fill in the middle of the mix tape. Then one by one stitch the brightly colored rainbow rows, until complete.

thread key

FINISHED MOTIF SIZE: 9 in (23 cm) w
X 12 in (30 cm) h

Color	Hanks	Type	Number	Name
	0.5	Appleton	992	Ivory
	0.25	Appleton	995	Red
	0.25	Appleton	474	Golden Yellow
	0.25	Appleton	253	Grass Green
	0.25	Appleton	481	Turquoise
	0.25	Appleton	456	Purple
	0.5	Appleton	993	Black

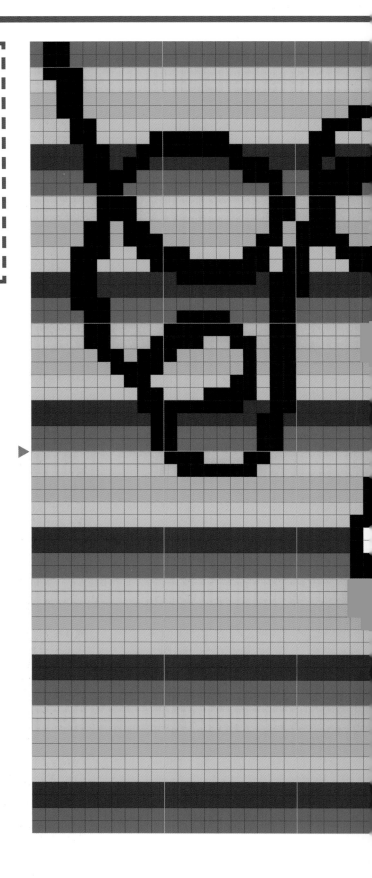

finishing

1 Block/press your finished tapestry, following the directions on page 150.

2 Trim the tapestry edges to leave a 1-in (2.5-cm) seam allowance around the edge of your work.

3 Follow the directions on page 156 for making up a pouch.

variations

● Refer to the chart on page 149 for yarn conversion to other tapestry yarn colors.

● I lined my tablet cover in a micro cotton cord. This also acts as a screen cleaner as you move the tablet in and out of the pouch.

● You may want to add a loop and button at the top to ensure your tablet does not fall out.

● You can adjust the size to accommodate a larger tablet simply by repeating the rainbow rows.

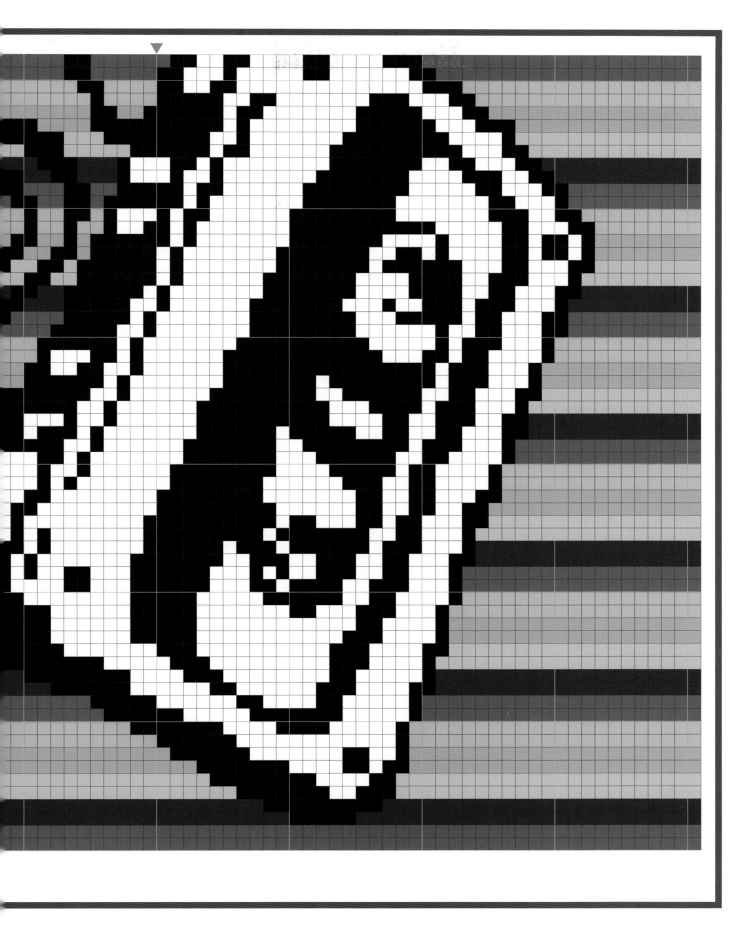

hot dog apron

14

I used to love old movies showing 50s drive-ins. With this design I have tried to capture that era and the pattern makes the perfect accompaniment to any summertime barbecue!

method

1 Prepare your base and find the middle by folding in half and half again.

2 Following the yarn key on page 70, find the color shown for bun.

3 Cut your thread to length, and then split the yarn in half, creating two lengths of three strands of yarn.

4 Thread your needle using the three strands and keep the others for later.

5 Count out from the middle to the bun area and begin to stitch, working left to right, following the chart.

6 Stitch the top half of the bun first, followed by the mustard, then the sausage, and then the other half of the bun. Lastly, stitch the rays one by one.

tools and materials

- 11-count Aida, 10 x 10 in (25 x 25 cm)
- DMC Stranded Cotton—see thread key on page 70
- Size 22 tapestry needle
- Threader (optional)
- Apron to attach pocket to
- Iron-on interlining, 10 x 10 in (25 x 25 cm)
- Matching sewing thread
- Sewing machine to make up

thread key

FINISHED MOTIF SIZE: 6½ in (16 cm) w
X 6½ in (16 cm) h

Color	Skein	Type	Number	Name
	1	DMC	321	Red
	0.10	DMC	444	Yellow
	0.25	DMC	801	Coffee Brown
	0.5	DMC	3864	Beige

finishing

1 Block/press your finished tapestry, following the directions on page 150, and trim any loose thread ends.

2 Place the interlining on the reverse side of your work (glue side down) and trim any excess interlining off so that it does not "glue" your ironing board. Cover with a dishtowel and press.

3 This process covers the back without the need for lining the pocket. If you prefer to line it you can follow the directions for lining an item on page 156.

4 Turn over the top edge by ¼ in (5 mm) and then ½ in (1 cm) and top stitch along the edge.

5 Fold over the other three edges by ½ in (1 cm), mitering the corners at the bottom.

6 Pin to your apron and then top stitch into place on three sides, leaving the top edge open.

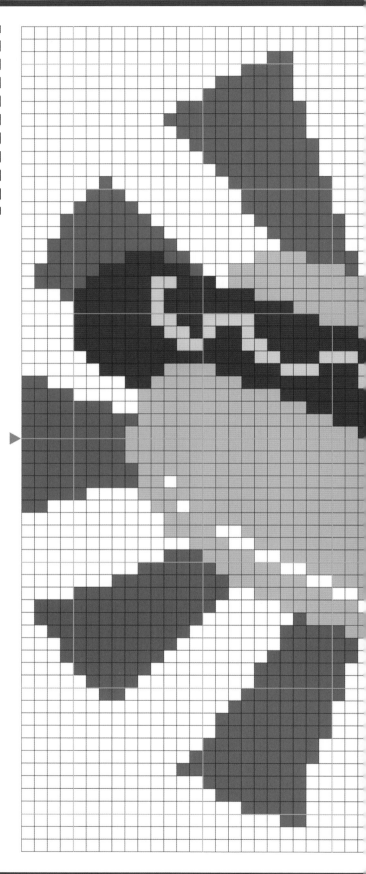

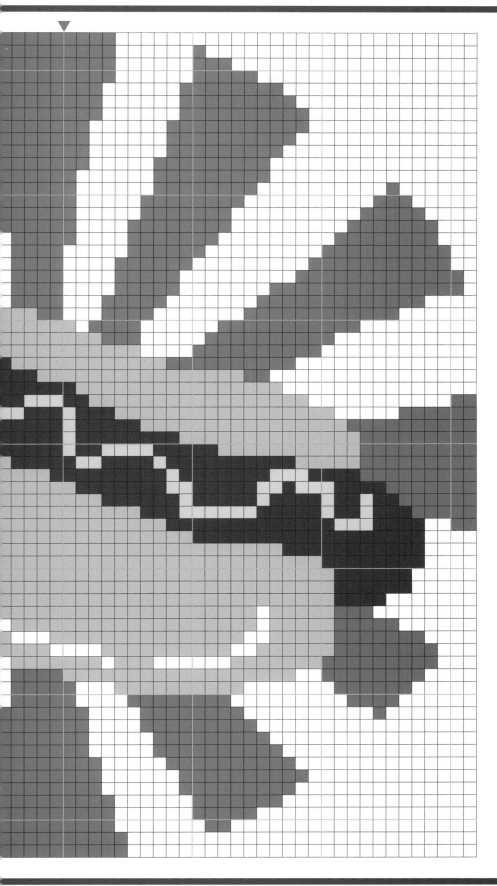

variations

● Refer to the chart on page 149 for yarn conversion to other tapestry yarn colors.

● If you don't want to make this into a pocket, simply omit stages 3–5, fold over all the edges as stage 6, then pin and stitch all sides onto your chosen apron.

● I think that this looks great with frou-frou vintage aprons, but works just as well on a more masculine apron.

● Alternatively, I think this would make a great pot holder. Simply make a template from your finished piece, cutting out a backing fabric and thick quilted liner, then binding the edges using a contrast trim.

15 mustache patch T-shirt

The humble mustache has had a revamp of late and has appeared on everything from mugs to T-shirts. I have created a simple badge which can be applied to a T-shirt or whatever you fancy.

tools and materials

- 28 evenweave, 8 x 8 in (20 x 20 cm)
- DMC Stranded Cotton—see thread key on page 75
- Size 22 tapestry needle
- Threader (optional)
- Hoop, 4 in (10 cm)
- Iron-on Interlining, 8 x 8 in (20 x 20 cm)
- Invisible embroidery pen
- Red Gutterman topstitching thread
- Sewing machine to make up

method

1 Prepare your base and find the middle by folding in half and half again.

2 Place in a hoop, making sure that the center is in the middle.

3 Cut your length of thread and then split the six strands into three, so you will have three lengths of two strands.

4 Thread your needle using two strands of the yarn.

5 Begin to stitch from the middle of the canvas, stitching over two threads (so that it is the equivalent of 14 count).

6 Working left to right, follow the chart until complete.

finishing

1 Block/press your finished tapestry, following the directions on page 150, and trim any loose thread ends.

2 Place the interlining on the reverse side of your work (glue side down) and trim any excess interlining off so that it does not "glue" your ironing board. Cover with a dishtowel and press. This process covers the back and stiffens your work, so that it is easier to work with.

3 Now use the template on page 153 and place it in the middle of your mustache.

4 Trace around the edge with your embroidery pen (I have used this because it disappears, but you could use a soft pencil instead, as this line will be covered with stitching.)

5 Set your sewing machine to a super-wide stitch with a tiny forward movement. This will create a wide stitch edge. You may want to test this on the outer edges of your fabric to get the stitch size and tension correct before starting on your work.

6 Slowly stitch around the circle so that you end up with a contrasting colored edge to your badge.

7 Using sharp scissors, trim around the edge against the stitching.

8 Your badge is now ready to sew onto a T-shirt, jacket, purse—whatever takes your fancy.

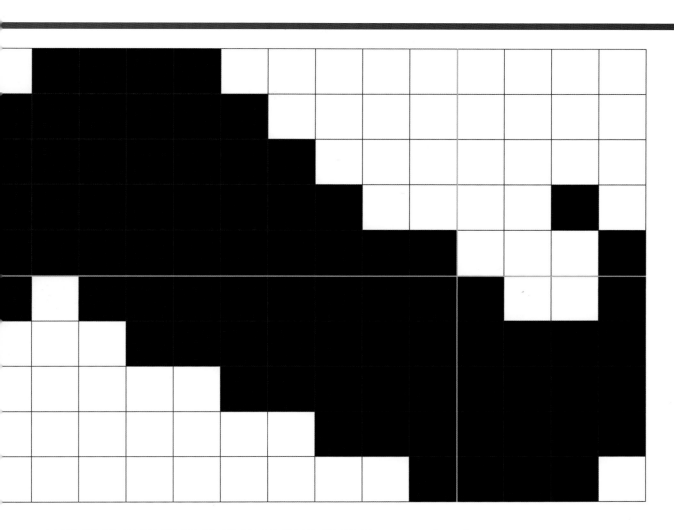

variations

● Refer to the chart on page 149 for yarn conversion to other tapestry yarn colors.

● You could stitch a few of these in different colors—or all together in a row.

● You could also use soluble canvas (8 count would be good), which will make the finished "tash" about 8 x 2¾ in (20 x 7 cm) in size. You can then stitch onto a pillowcase, or dishtowel … the list is endless. Soluble canvas can be your friend and makes a little motif go a long way.

16 heart on your sleeve badge

If you (like me) wear your heart on your sleeve then this badge is a perfect mini stitch project. It is super-versatile and can be added to bags or clothing, or simply given as a gift as a mini love token.

stitch stats

stitches: 32 x 27
yarn: Appleton tapestry wool
base: 7-count canvas
skill level: 1

method

1 Prepare your base and find the middle by folding in half and half again.

2 Following the yarn key on page 78, find the color shown for the heart.

3 Thread your needle using a single strand of the yarn.

4 Begin to stitch from the middle of the canvas—working left to right, following the chart—stitch the heart.

5 Follow with the arrow, then the border and finally fill in the ivory background color.

tools and materials

- 7-count canvas, 8 x 8 in (20 x 20 cm)
- 4 Ply Appleton Tapestry Yarn—see thread key on page 78
- Size 18 tapestry needle
- Threader (optional)
- Matching sewing thread

thread key

FINISHED MOTIF SIZE: 5 in (12 cm) w
X 4 in (10 cm) h

Color	Hanks	Type	Number	Name
	0.25	Appleton	992	Ivory
	0.25	Appleton	995	Red
	0.25	Appleton	481	Turquoise
	0.1	Appleton	993	Black

finishing

1 Block/press your finished tapestry, following the directions on page 150.

2 Trim the tapestry edges to leave a ⅝-in (1.5-cm) seam allowance around the edge of your work.

3 The finished work is very forgiving. You can lightly steam the back of the badge, then fold in the corners, then each of the sides, pressing as you go.

4 Your badge is ready to go. Simply pin your badge onto your chosen jacket and slip stitch around the edge.

variations

● Refer to the chart on page 149 for yarn conversion to other tapestry yarn colors.
● Instead of sewing directly onto a jacket, you can instead make a classic pin badge.
● When finishing, at step 4, measure and cut a piece of felt the same size as your finished badge, then slip stitch this onto the back.
● Sew on a pin fastening and you have a badge that can be pinned onto anything.

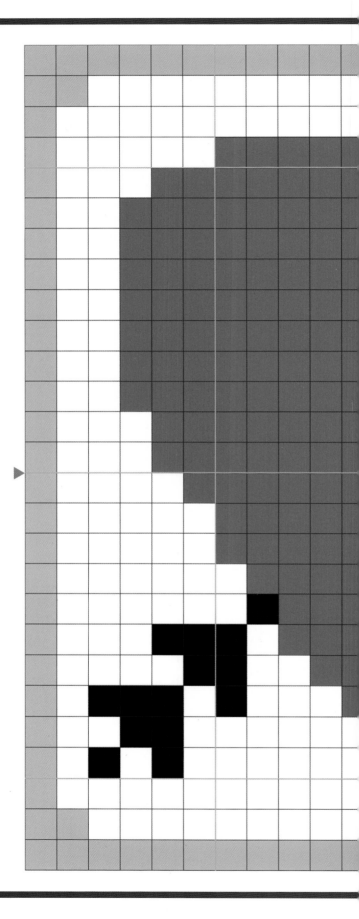

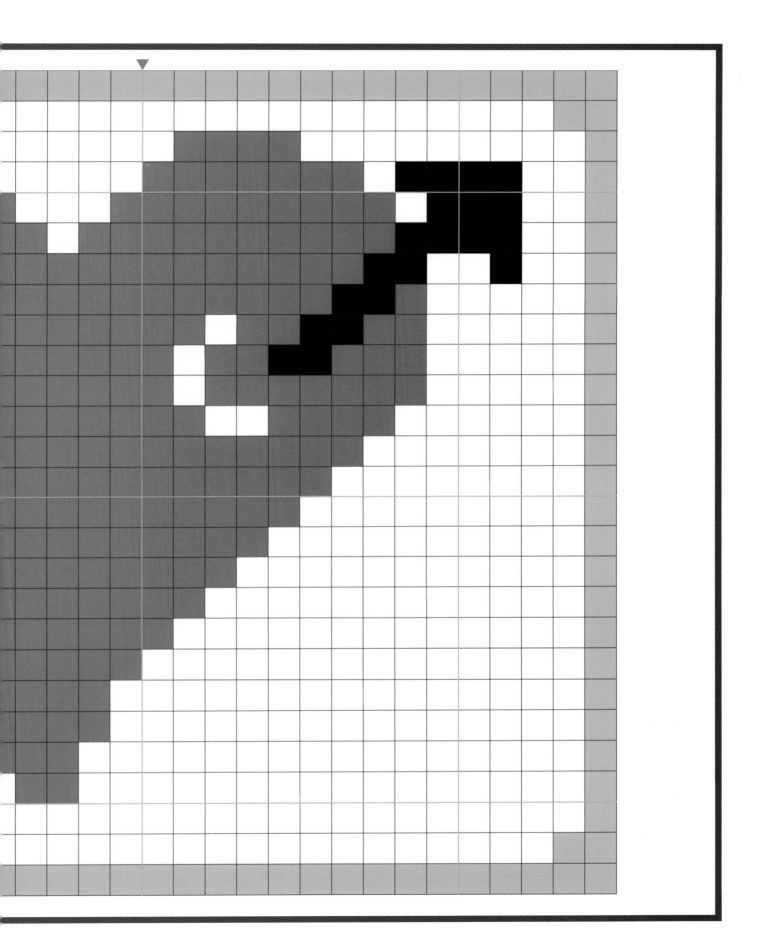

17 big bow clutch

This elegant purse is a combination of girly charm and graphic modernism. Its bold, bright statement is a perfect addition to any day or evening celebration. It is also a great quick stitch project.

stitch stats

stitches: 62 x 77
yarn: Appleton tapestry wool
base: 7-count canvas
skill level: 2

method

1 Prepare your base and find the middle by folding in half and half again.

2 Following the yarn key on page 82, find the color shown for the bow outline.

3 Thread your needle using a single strand of the yarn.

4 Count out from the middle of the canvas to the bow outline and start to stitch it, working up and down following the chart.

5 Once the outline is complete fill in the bow, followed by the edging at the end adjacent to the bow.

6 Start to work the pale pattern until it is complete, followed by the other edge. Finally, fill in the background.

tools and materials

- 7-count canvas, 14 x 16 in (35 x 40 cm)
- 4-ply Appleton Tapestry Yarn—see thread key on page 82
- Size 18 tapestry needle
- Threader (optional)
- Backing fabric, 2 x 12 x 20 in (30 x 50 cm) pieces of fabric
- Matching sewing thread
- Sewing machine to make up

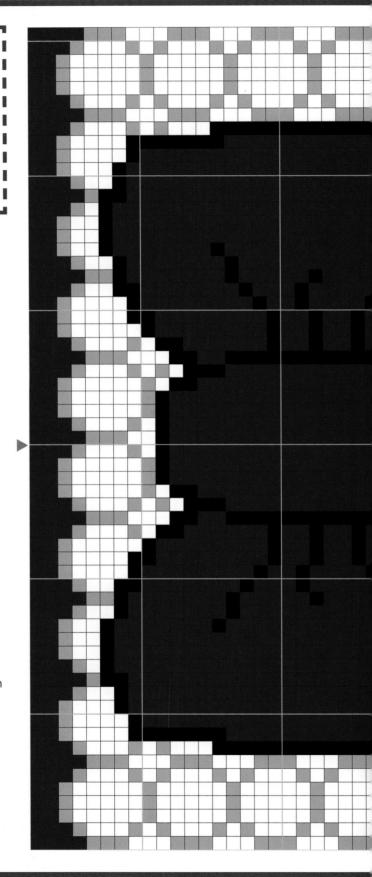

thread key

FINISHED MOTIF SIZE: 8½ in (22.5 cm) w
X 11 in (28 cm) h (fold in half for purse)

Color	Hanks	Type	Number	Name
☐	1	Appleton	992	Ivory
◼	0.5	Appleton	456	Purple
◼	0.1	Appleton	993	Black
◼	0.5	Appleton	885	Lilac

finishing

1 Block/press your finished tapestry, following the directions on page 150.

2 Trim the tapestry edges to leave a 1-in (2.5-cm) seam allowance around the edge of your work.

3 Follow the directions on page 157 for making up the purse.

variations

● Refer to the chart on page 149 for yarn conversion to other tapestry yarn colors.
● This is what I call an infinity pattern—you can keep going until you run out of canvas. The circles background can go on and on.
● This bow would also make a fabulous pillow. Decide on the size of the pillow (eg 16 x 16 in/40 x 40 cm) and keep the bow at the bottom or put it in the middle and then stitch outward with the circles repeating until you have the pillow size required, edging in the darker color on all four sides.
● Then follow the directions on page 155 on how to make a simple pillow.

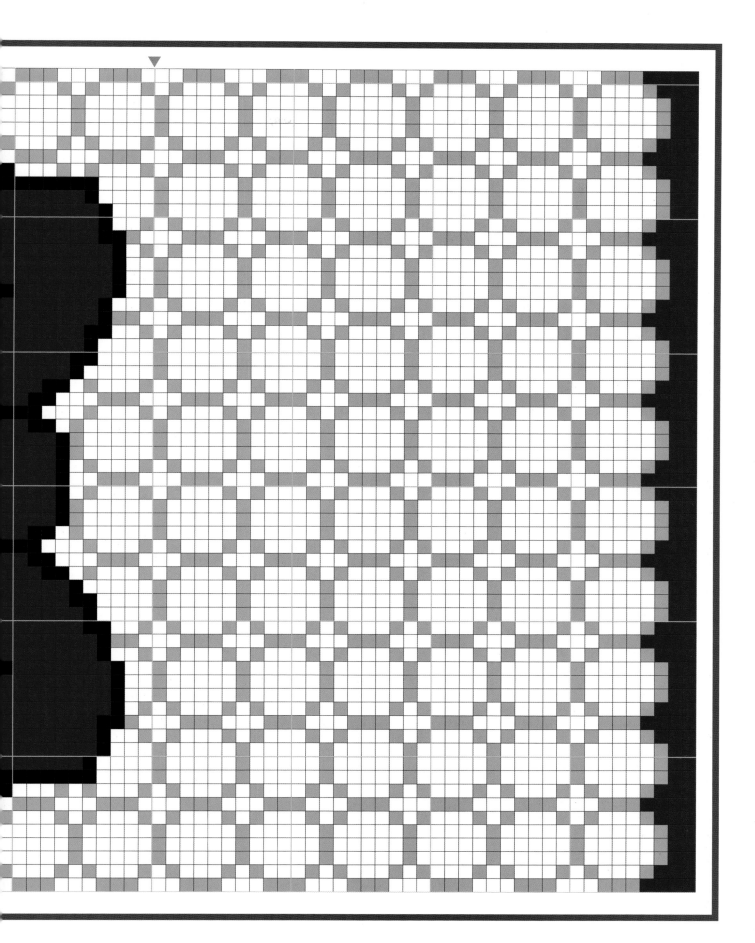

18 lipstick makeup purse

There is nothing like a good girl's night out with friends. When I was single we used to have just as much fun getting ready together as we did when we were out; this purse is my homage to those nights.

stitch stats

stitches: 75 x 51
yarn: Appleton tapestry wool
base: 7-count canvas
skill level: 2

tools and materials

- 7-count canvas, 16 x 12 in (40 x 30 cm)
- 4-ply Appleton Tapestry Yarn—see thread key on page 86
- Size 18 tapestry needle
- Threader (optional)
- Backing fabric, 16 x 12 in (40 x 30 cm)
- Lining fabric, 2 x 16 x 12 in (40 x 30 cm)
- Colored plastic zipper, 4 in (10 cm)
- Few 8-in (20-cm) strands of ¼-in (5-mm) ribbon or rope to decorate (optional)
- Matching sewing thread
- Sewing machine to make up

method

1 Prepare your base and find the middle by folding in half and half again.

2 Following the yarn key on page 86, find the color shown for the lipstick.

3 Thread your needle using a single strand of the yarn.

4 Begin to stitch from the middle of the canvas—working up and down, following the chart. Stitch the lipstick first, then the lipstick case.

5 Work on the diagonal stripes—I always find that it is easier to complete the darker one first.

6 When they are complete, finish with the lighter stripe.

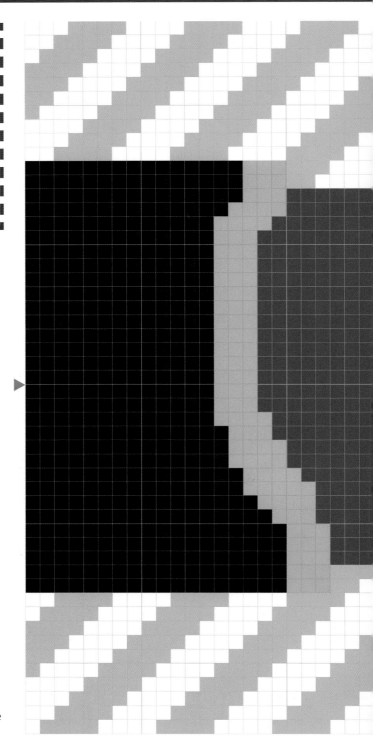

thread key

FINISHED MOTIF SIZE: 10¾ in (27 cm) w
X 7½ in (19 cm) h

Color	Hanks	Type	Number	Name
	0.5	Appleton	992	Ivory
	0.1	Appleton	474	Golden Yellow
	0.5	Appleton	803	Fuchsia
	0.5	Appleton	483	Dark Turquoise
	0.25	Appleton	993	Black

finishing

1 Block/press your finished tapestry, following the directions on page 150.

2 Trim the tapestry edges to leave a 1-in (2.5-cm) seam allowance around the edge of your work.

3 Follow the directions on page 157 for making up a zipped pouch.

4 If you want to add the ribbon flourish to the zipper, simply take two 8-in (20-cm) lengths of ¼-in (5-mm) ribbon and fold them in half. Thread the loop end through the zipper and then thread the loose ends through these loops, and pull taut.

variations

● Refer to the chart on page 149 for yarn conversion to other tapestry yarn colors.
● This is another infinity project which can be easily converted into a pillow or larger piece by repeating the stripe pattern to as big as you like (see page 82).

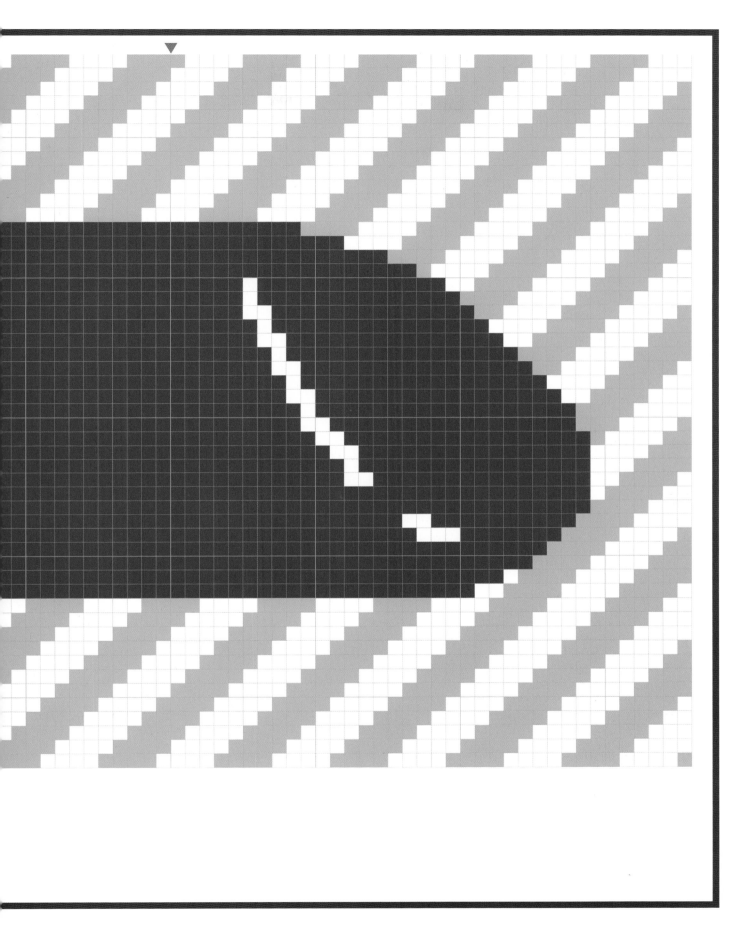

orange segment purse

This mini purse is a mouthwateringly easy quick project to whip up in your spare time. It can be easily adapted to produce a rainbow of fruity flavors to give as a gift or simply keep for your spare change.

stitch stats

stitches: 34 x 19
yarn: Appleton tapestry wool
base: 7-count canvas
skill level: 1

method

1 Prepare your base and find the middle by folding in half and half again.

2 Following the yarn key on page 90 find the color shown for the pith.

3 Thread your needle using a single strand of the yarn.

4 Counting from the middle, stitch this pith color first, then stitch the orange, and finally, the brown end.

tools and materials

- 7-count canvas, 9 x 6¾ in (23 x 17 cm)
- 4-ply Appleton Tapestry Yarn—see thread key on page 90
- Size 18 tapestry needle
- Threader (optional)
- Lining fabric, 2 x 9 x 6¾ in (23 x 17 cm)
- Backing fabric 9 x 6¾ in (23 x 17 cm)
- Mini colored zipper, 5½ in (14 cm)
- Matching sewing thread
- Sewing machine to make up

finishing

1 Block/press your finished tapestry, following the directions on page 150.

2 Trim the tapestry edges to leave a ½-in (1-cm) seam allowance around the edge of your work.

3 Make a template following the directions on pages 152–3. Cut out two linings and one backing fabric.

4 Follow the directions on page 157 for making up the zippered pouch.

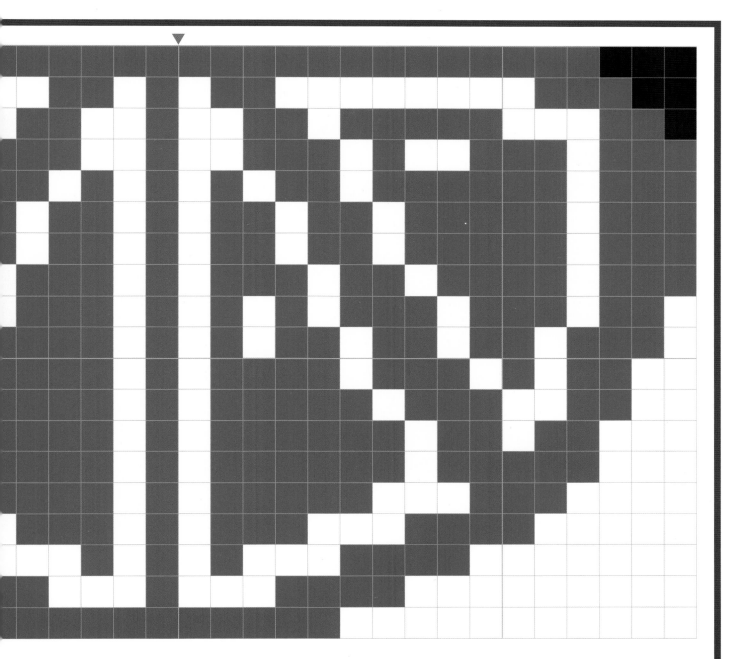

variations

● Refer to the chart on page 149 for yarn conversion to other tapestry yarn colors. You can make this up in Yellow for a lemon and Grass Green for a lime.

● You can also repeat the pattern on the back side instead of the backing fabric, so that the cross stitch is seen on the front and back sides.

20 sleep tight mask

"Night night, sleep tight" and this cutest of sleep masks will ensure that you get the most stylish shut eye, whether you are on a plane or train, in an automobile, or simply in your boudoir.

stitch stats

stitches: 61 x 25
yarn: Appleton tapestry wool
base: 7-count canvas
skill level: 1

method

1 Prepare your base and find the middle by folding in half and half again.

2 Following the yarn key on page 94, find the color shown for the eyelashes.

3 Thread your needle using a single strand of the yarn.

4 Count out from the middle and begin to stitch the eyelashes—stitching up and down, trying to keep your stitches in the same direction.

5 Start to stitch the stripes. You can take these one at a time, or do all of the pink first and then all of the ivory.

6 Finally, complete the pink border around the edge of the mask.

tools and materials

- 7-count canvas, 14 x 8 in (35 x 20 cm)
- 4-ply Appleton Tapestry Yarn—see thread key on page 94
- Size 18 tapestry needle
- Threader (optional)
- Backing fabric, 14 x 8 in (35 x 20 cm)
- 1¼-in (3-cm) wide colored elastic, about 20 in (50 cm) long
- Matching sewing thread
- Sewing machine to make up

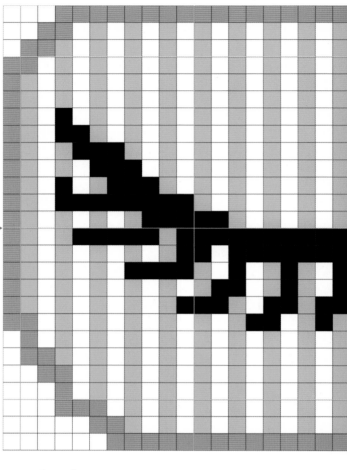

thread key

FINISHED MOTIF SIZE: 9 in (23 cm) w
X 4 in (10 cm) h

Color	Hanks	Type	Number	Name
☐	0.25	Appleton	992	Ivory
▨	0.25	Appleton	943	Pink
▨	0.25	Appleton	945	Dark Pink
■	0.1	Appleton	993	Black

finishing

1 Block/press your finished tapestry, following the directions on page 150.

2 Trim the tapestry edges to leave a ½-in (1-cm) seam allowance around the edge of your work.

3 Using the template directions on pages 152–3, cut out the backing fabric.

4 Take one end of the elastic and place it on the tapestry, so that the raw edge is aligned with the raw edge of the tapestry (right sides together). Topstitch this in place.

5 At this point check the length of the elastic and how tight you want it. Place the right side of the stitched mask over your eyes (or a willing friend's) and take the elastic around your head to see how long you want it to be.

6 Again, place the right sides together and topstitch this in place.

7 Trim off any excess, then place the backing fabric on the mask, right sides together.

8 Stitch around (making sure that the elastic is tucked in the middle), leaving an opening at the top for turning out.

9 Make several "nips" with your scissors around the nose bridge area so that it does not pucker. Turn out, press, and slip stitch the opening closed.

variations

● Refer to the chart on page 149 for yarn conversion to other tapestry yarn colors.
● This works well changed into other colors, or you could simply stitch the background in one plain color.
● You could cover your elastic in a contrasting fabric. Just make up a fabric tube that is 1.5 times longer and 5 mm wider than the elastic, and thread elastic through before inserting into the mask edges.

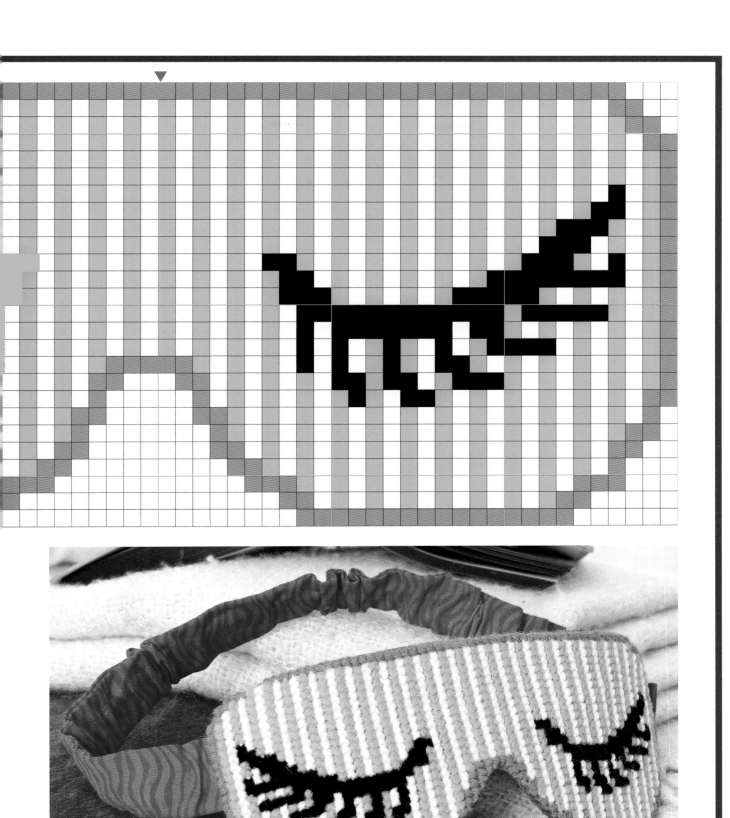

21 retro phone case

There was a time when dialing a long phone number took ages as you waited for the dial to spin back around after each number. This project is a real old-meets-new nostalgic piece.

stitch stats

stitches: 25 x 37
yarn: Appleton tapestry wool
base: 7-count canvas
skill level: 2

method

1 Prepare your base and find the middle by folding in half and half again.

2 Following the yarn key on page 98, find the color shown for the heart.

3 Thread your needle using a single strand of the yarn.

4 Begin to stitch from the middle of the canvas—working up and down, following the chart to complete the heart.

5 Continue outward, stitching the dial and then the phone.

6 Lastly, complete the stripes, stitching a row at a time.

tools and materials

- 7-count canvas, 8 x 10 in (20 x 25 cm)
- 4-ply Appleton Tapestry Yarn—see thread key on page 98
- Size 18 tapestry needle
- Threader (optional)
- Backing fabric, 8 x 10 in (20 x 25 cm)
- Lining fabric, 2 x 8 x 10 in (20 x 25 cm)
- Matching sewing thread
- Sewing machine to make up

thread key

FINISHED MOTIF SIZE: 3½ in (9 cm) w
X 5½ in (14 cm) h

Color	Hanks	Type	Number	Name
☐	0.15	Appleton	992	Ivory
■	0.1	Appleton	995	Red
☐	0.25	Appleton	553	Yellow
■	0.25	Appleton	993	Black

finishing

1 Block/press your finished tapestry, following the directions on page 150.

2 Trim the tapestry edges to leave a 1-in (2.5-cm) seam allowance around the edge of your work.

3 Follow the directions on page 156 for making up a lined pouch.

variations

● Refer to the chart on page 149 for yarn conversion to other tapestry yarn colors.
● You could change the heart to a mini stitched letter in cross stitch or topstitch to personalize your case.
● Or stitch the stripes in any color you fancy.
● Blackberries and iphones fit into this case—and you can always extend out the stripes for a larger device.

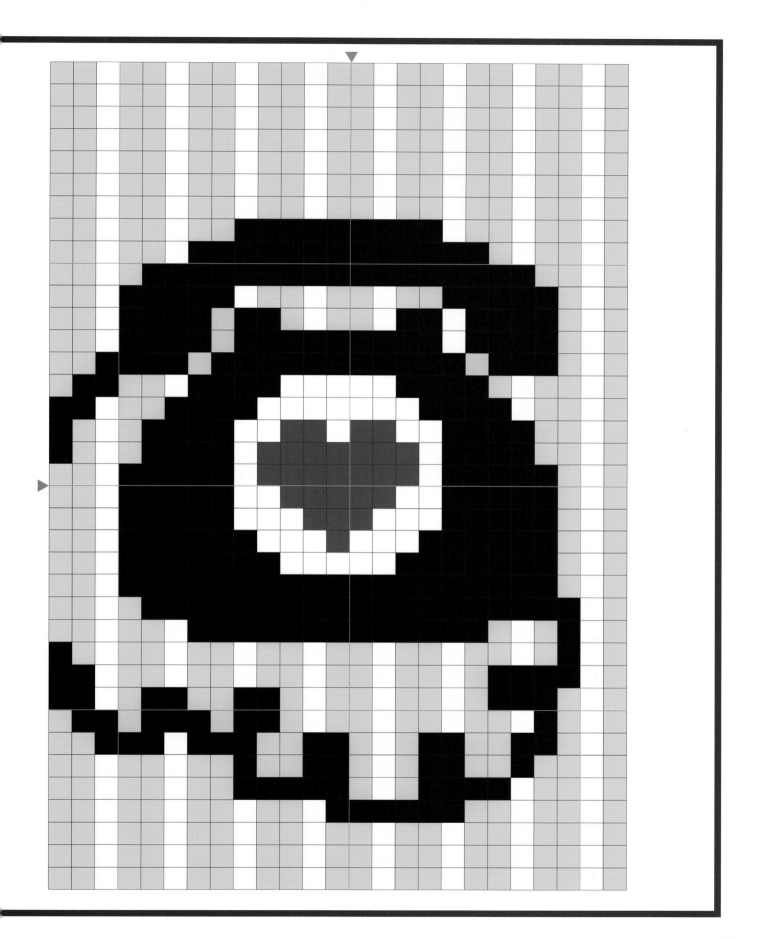

WHALE OF A WALL

My grandma's walls were always covered in framed cross stitch scenes, and this is perhaps the most traditional method of finishing off your work. This chapter is about the wow factor, and I have created a collection of projects, both big and small, to make a huge impression on your walls. So whether it's a mini bird or a piece of oversized flatware, there is something for everyone to hang up on the wall and admire.

peony bloom picture

22

Peonies are my favorite flower as their colorful, casual abundance in June is a sight to cherish. This project captures one of the varieties I love, to grace your walls all year long.

stitch stats

stitches: 86 x 86
yarn: Appleton tapestry wool
base: 5-count canvas
skill level: 1

method

1 Prepare your base and find the middle by folding in half and half again.

2 Check the chart on page 105 and following the yarn key on page 104, find the color shown in the middle section.

3 Thread your needle using two strands of the yarn, or use one strand folded in half to begin with the quick start method on page 146.

4 Begin to stitch from the middle of the canvas—working left to right.

5 Complete each petal individually, continuing to stitch left to right along the rows.

6 Work your way outward to complete the petals, stems, and leaves, then fill in the ivory background last.

tools and materials

- 5-count canvas, 27½ x 27½ in (70 x 70 cm)
- 4-ply Appleton Tapestry Yarn—see thread key on page 104
- Size 14 tapestry needle
- Threader (optional)
- Frame

thread key

FINISHED MOTIF SIZE: 20 in (50 cm) w
X 20 in (50 cm) h

Color	Hanks	Type	Number	Name
	3	Appleton	992	Ivory
	0.25	Appleton	474	Golden Yellow
	0.5	Appleton	253	Grass Green
	0.25	Appleton	255	Dark Grass
	1.5	Appleton	803	Fuschia
	1.5	Appleton	943	Pink
	0.25	Appleton	187	Brown

finishing

1 Block/press your finished tapestry, following the directions on page 150.

2 As the 5 count is such a large count base it is very easy for the tapestry to distort, but it is just as easy to steam it back into shape.

3 Refer to the information on page 151 about framing your piece when finished.

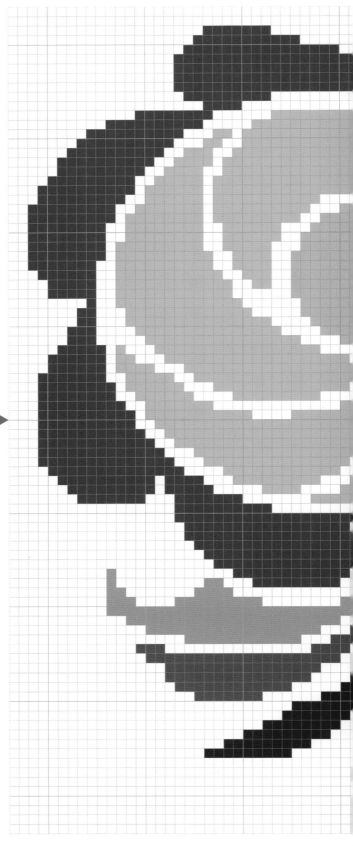

variations

● Refer to the chart on page 149 for yarn conversion to other tapestry yarn colors.

● This project also works very well as a pillow or seat cover.

● You can stitch it in 7 count for a smaller pillow (about 12 in/30 cm square when finished), if you like.

23 flower tile picture

This is a supersized single flower version of the retro bloom pillow on page 30. The two projects work brilliantly in unison, and this single bloom is a perfect project for beginners.

method

1 Prepare your base and find the middle by folding in half and half again.

2 Check the chart on page 109 and following the yarn key on page 108, find the color shown in the middle section.

3 Thread your needle using two strands of the yarn, or use one strand folded in half to start with the quick start method on page 146.

4 Begin to stitch from the middle of the canvas—working left to right.

5 Complete the middle and then each element individually, continuing to stitch left to right along the rows.

6 Work your way outward, then fill in the ivory background last.

tools and materials

- 5-count canvas, 20 x 20 in (50 x 50 cm)
- 4-ply Appleton Tapestry Yarn—see thread key on page 108
- Size 14 tapestry needle
- Threader (optional)
- Frame

thread key

FINISHED MOTIF SIZE: 12 in (30 cm) w
X 12 in (30 cm) h

Color	Hanks	Type	Number	Name
	2	Appleton	992	Ivory
	0.5	Appleton	995	Red
	0.5	Appleton	445	Orange
	0.5	Appleton	474	Golden Yellow
	0.5	Appleton	253	Grass Green
	1	Appleton	481	Turquoise
	1	Appleton	943	Pink
	0.5	Appleton	456	Purple

finishing

1 Block/press your finished tapestry, following the directions on page 150.

2 As the 5-count is such a large count base it is very easy for the tapestry to distort, but it is just as easy to steam it back into shape.

3 Refer to the information on page 151 about framing your piece when finished.

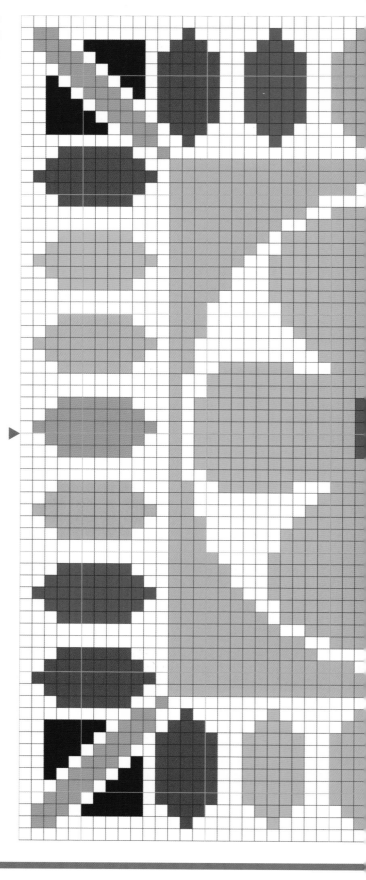

variations

● Refer to the chart on page 149 for yarn conversion to other tapestry yarn colors.

● This works equally well as a pillow. Refer to page 155 for information on how to make a simple pillow.

big love picture

This luscious project is a labor of love. The big, colorful floral stitched letters will make a real statement of affection on any wall, and the picture is perfect given to someone you love as a present.

stitch stats

stitches: 236 x 82
yarn: Appleton tapestry wool
base: 7-count canvas
skill level: 3

tools and materials

- 7-count canvas 39 x 17³⁄₄ in (100 x 45 cm)
- 4-ply Appleton Tapestry Yarn—see thread key on page 112
- Size 18 tapestry needle
- Threader (optional)
- Frame

method

1 Prepare your base and find the middle by folding in half and half again.

2 Check the chart on pages 112–3 and following the yarn key on page 112, find the color shown on the outside of the letter "O."

3 Thread your needle using a single strand of the yarn.

4 Count out from the middle point to the edge of the O and start to stitch, trying to keep your stitches in the same direction.

5 You can either continue with the same color, or keep swapping between the colors within the "O" until it is complete.

6 Continue with each letter individually, making sure that your stitches flow in the same direction.

7 Complete the edge border, then fill in the ivory last, continuing to stitch left to right along the rows.

thread key

FINISHED MOTIF SIZE: 33½ in (85 cm) w
X 12 in (30 cm) h

Color	Hanks	Type	Number	Name
	3	Appleton	992	Ivory
	0.5	Appleton	995	Red
	0.25	Appleton	445	Orange
	0.25	Appleton	553	Yellow
	0.25	Appleton	474	Golden Yellow
	0.25	Appleton	253	Grass Green
	0.5	Appleton	255	Dark Green
	0.25	Appleton	325	Marine
	0.25	Appleton	481	Turquoise
	0.25	Appleton	483	Dark Turquoise
	0.75	Appleton	943	Pink
	0.5	Appleton	945	Dark Pink
	0.5	Appleton	456	Purple
	0.25	Appleton	885	Lilac
	0.25	Appleton	187	Brown

finishing

1 Block/press your finished tapestry, following the directions on page 150.

2 Refer to the information on page 151 about framing your piece when finished.

variations

● Refer to the chart on page 149 for yarn conversion to other tapestry yarn colors. Make sure that you use the same kind of yarn within the whole piece.

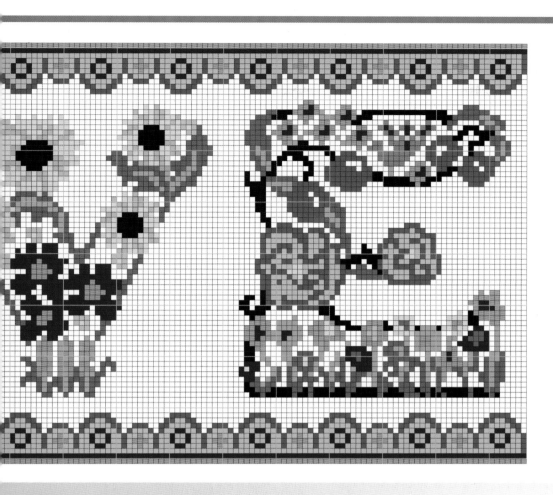

flatware hanging

Supersized rainbow retro flatware makes a huge statement on any wall, but particularly in your kitchen or living area. This project uses straps to hang on the wall, so there is no need for a frame.

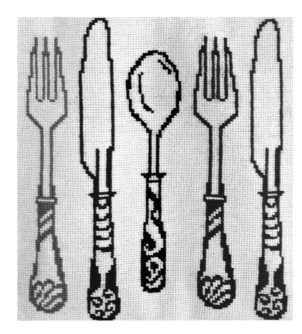

stitch stats

stitches: 266 x 134
yarn: Appleton tapestry wool
base: 7-count canvas
skill level: 3

method

1 Prepare your base and find the middle by folding in half and half again.

2 Check the chart on page 116 and following the yarn key on page 116, find the color shown for the fork just to the right of the middle.

3 Thread your needle using a single 4-ply strand of the yarn.

4 Count out from the middle to the fork, then begin to stitch and complete the fork.

5 Continue working each piece of flatware, following the chart and trying to keep the stitching in the same direction.

6 When you have completed all the pieces of flatware fill in the blank areas, making sure that you keep the stitching going in the same direction.

tools and materials

- 7-count canvas, 43 x 23½ in (110 x 60 cm)
- 4-ply Appleton Tapestry Yarn —see thread key on page 116
- Size 18 tapestry needle
- Threader (optional)
- Backing fabric, 41 x 21½ in (105 x 55 cm)
- Matching sewing thread
- 6½ ft (2 m) x 1½-in (4-cm) wide tape for hanging straps
- 3 ft (1 m) x ¾-in (2-cm) doweling rod
- Ribbon or trim to hang your rod
- Sewing machine to make up

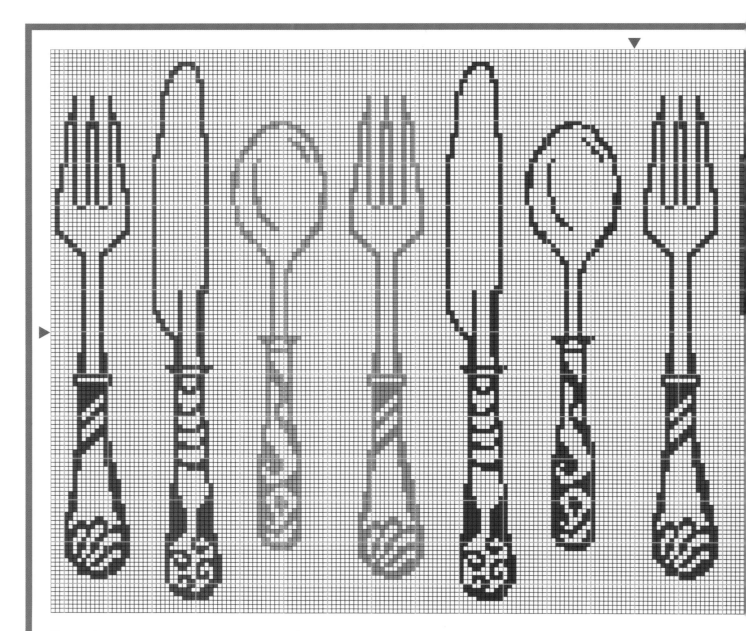

Color	Hanks	Type	Number	Name
	10	Appleton	992	Ivory
	0.5	Appleton	995	Red
	0.5	Appleton	445	Orange
	0.5	Appleton	474	Golden Yellow
	0.5	Appleton	253	Grass Green
	0.5	Appleton	486	Kingfisher
	0.5	Appleton	803	Fuchsia

finishing

1 Block/press your finished tapestry, following the directions on page 150.

2 Trim the tapestry edges to leave a 1-in (2.5-cm) seam allowance around the edge of your work.

3 Cut a paper pattern to the backing fabric size, and cut out the backing fabric.

4 Next, make the hanging loops for the rod. Cut the wide tape into five pieces of equal length, each 1.3 ft (40 cm). Fold each of them in half.

variations

● Refer to the chart on page 149 for yarn conversion.

● You could change the colors of the flatware to match your kitchen color scheme, or downsize the project by stitching on 14-count Aida with stranded cotton. This will approximately halve its finished size.

5 Pin, then baste the loops to the back of the tapestry piece (with the loops facing inward toward the middle of the tapestry, placing one in the middle, one at either end, and the last two between.

6 Place the tapestry and the fabric right side together, and pin.

7 Sew around the edge of the tapestry, starting at the middle of the bottom side, until you have stitched around the whole tapestry, leaving a gap of 10 in (25 cm) at the bottom. **Note:** Keep the tapes straight as you stitch around the tapestry, otherwise they will not hang straight.

8 Turn the right way out, ensuring that you push out the four corners. Lightly steam flat, using a damp dishtowel.

9 Slip stitch the opening closed using the directions on page 154.

10 Lightly press, using a damp dishtowel, then thread the doweling rod through the loops at the top and hang using the ribbon.

26 birdy picture

This cute bird has a rainbow fantail. I stitched this as a quick project to show how you can stitch over multiple threads on evenweave to get supersize results. It also works well on tapestry or Aida.

stitch stats

stitches: 50 x 52
yarn: DMC stranded cotton
base: 28 evenweave—stitched over 2 stitches (14 HPI)
skill level: 2

tools and materials

- 28-count evenweave 10 x 10 in (25 x 25 cm)
- Stranded Cotton DMC Yarn—see thread key on page 120
- Size 22 tapestry needle
- Threader (optional)
- Hoop
- Frame

method

1 Prepare your base and find the middle by folding in half and half again. Hoop and mark your center spot.

2 Check the chart on page 121 and following the yarn key on page 120, find the color shown in the middle section.

3 Thread your needle using two strands (out of the six strands) of the yarn, or use one strand folded in half to start with the quick start method on page 146.

4 Begin to stitch from the middle of the base—working left to right.

5 Work your stitches over two threads of the base, so that the stitches are twice as big. Once you have got going it will be easy to see the pattern and size emerging.

6 Complete the middle and then complete each element individually, continuing to stitch left to right along the rows, and working your way outward.

thread key

FINISHED MOTIF SIZE: 4 in (10 cm) w
X 4 in (10 cm) h

Color	Skein	Type	Number	Name
	1	DMC	898	Brown
	1	DMC	956	Pink
	1	DMC	321	Red
	1	DMC	959	Turquoise
	1	DMC	907	Green
	1	DMC	444	Yellow
	1	DMC	550	Purple
	1	DMC	606	Orange

finishing

1 Block/press your finished stitching, following the directions on page 150.

2 Refer to the information on page 151 about framing your piece when finished.

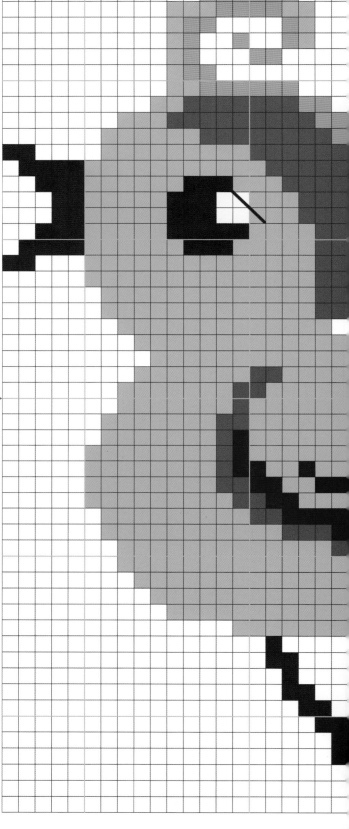

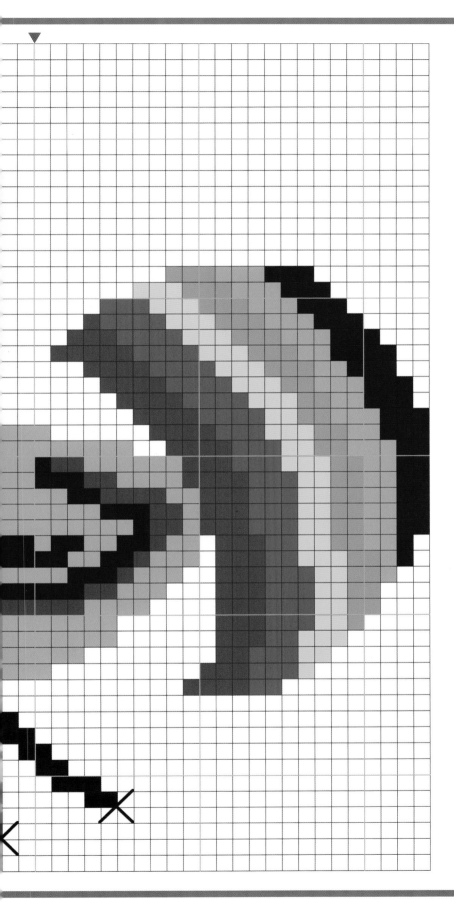

variations

● Refer to the chart on page 149 for yarn conversion to other tapestry yarn colors.

● This works equally well on tapestry 7 count, and will be about twice as big. You can use the yarn convertor on page 149, but remember you will need to add in a background yarn color like Ivory.

cracked egg picture

This fun project is a perfect quick-stitch design for your kitchen wall. Alternatively, it is a great piece for children and beginners to learn how to cross stitch.

stitch stats

stitches: 41 x 53
yarn: Appleton tapestry wool
base: 7-count canvas
skill level: 1

method

1 Find the middle of your tapestry canvas by folding in half and half again.

2 Check the chart on page 125 and following the yarn key on page 124, find the color of the top stripe of the egg cup.

3 Thread your needle using a single 4-ply strand of the yarn.

4 Count up from the middle to the top of the egg cup stripe, and begin to stitch—working left to right, following the chart.

5 Work your way down the egg cup, then complete the egg.

6 Stitch the background color to complete the project.

tools and materials

- 7-count canvas 12 x 14 in (30 x 35 cm)
- 4-ply Appleton Tapestry Yarn—see thread key on page 124
- Size 18 tapestry needle
- Threader (optional)
- Frame

variations

● Refer to the chart on page 149 for yarn conversion to other tapestry yarn colors.

thread key

FINISHED MOTIF SIZE: 6 in (15 cm) w
X 8 in (20 cm) h

Color	Hanks	Type	Number	Name
	0.1	Appleton	992	Ivory
	0.5	Appleton	995	Red
	0.1	Appleton	984	Eggshell
	0.1	Appleton	553	Yellow
	0.1	Appleton	486	Kingfisher

finishing

1 Block/press your finished tapestry, following the directions on page 150.

2 Refer to the information on page 151 about framing your piece when finished.

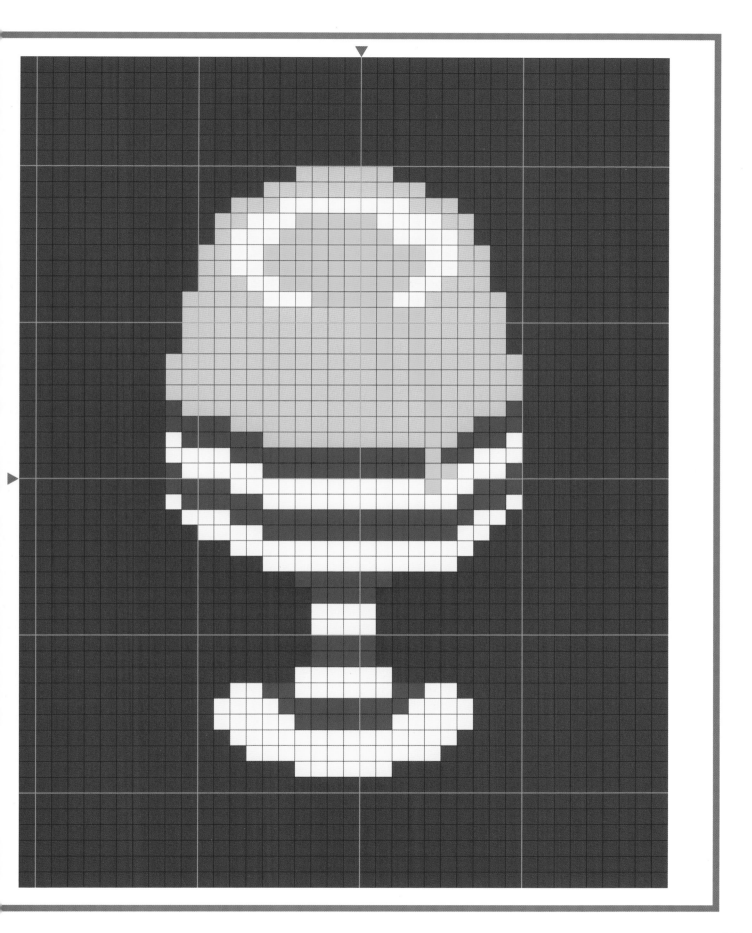

COLOSSAL CHRISTMAS

Christmas is my favorite time of year and it is an excuse to go mad on decorations, clash colors, and let out your inner creative demon. But perhaps my most treasured thing about Christmas is the memories, and every year our family create new traditions. So I have created a mix-and-match collection of Christmas pieces to stitch and cherish year after year.

28 noel bunting

Bunting has become a party decorating staple. Here, I have created something in supersize stitches especially for the festive season—perfect for hanging over your mantle or across a doorway.

stitch stats

stitches: 70 x 50 shaped each
yarn: Appleton tapestry wool
base: 7-count canvas
skill level: 2

method

1 Prepare your base and find the middle by folding in half and half again.

2 Following the yarn key on page 131, find the color shown for the letter "N."

3 Thread your needle using a single strand of the yarn.

4 Check the chart on page 130 and counting out the number of blank spaces from the middle, start stitching the N flag.

5 Stitch from right to left, stitching one whole flag at a time.

6 Continue stitching outward, one flag at a time, to complete the canvas. Make sure to leave the blank gaps (as shown on the chart) between each bunting flag as a seam allowance for the finished items.

tools and materials

- 7-count canvas, 26 x 14 in (65 x 35 cm), I have laid out chart to stitch all bunting together and maximize use of your canvas; trim later
- 4-ply Appleton Tapestry Yarn—see thread key on page 131
- Size 18 tapestry needle
- Threader (optional)
- Backing fabric, 26 x 14-in (66 x 35-cm) if you lay out same as tapestry or 8½ in (22 cm) width x 12 in (30 cm) length per bunting
- Matching sewing thread
- Ribbon or trim to hang
- Sewing machine to make up

finishing

1 Block/press your finished tapestry, following the directions on page 150.

2 Cut out each individual bunting, making sure that you leave a ½-in (1-cm) seam allowance around the edge of each flag.

3 Make a template using the instructions on page 152, then cut out six pieces of your chosen backing fabric.

4 Place each piece of bunting tapestry and fabric right sides together and pin.

5 Stitch along the two long edges of the flag, making sure that you keep right on the edge of the tapestry, so as not to get any "grinning."

6 Repeat the process in step 5 above with all the bunting tapestry pieces.

7 Trim the pointed edge of the bunting off (removing the bulk of the seam), leaving about ¼ in (5 mm).

8 Turn each flag the right way around and press (poking out the point with a pencil or knitting needle). Fold in the top edges, then press and pin.

9 Cut the length of trim required to hang across your mantle (I used 8 ft/2.5 m).

10 Organize the flags evenly across your trim in the correct order, leaving about a 2-in (5-cm) gap between each bunting flag, then pin.

11 Slip stitch (see page 154) each piece of bunting onto your trim. Your bunting is now ready to hang.

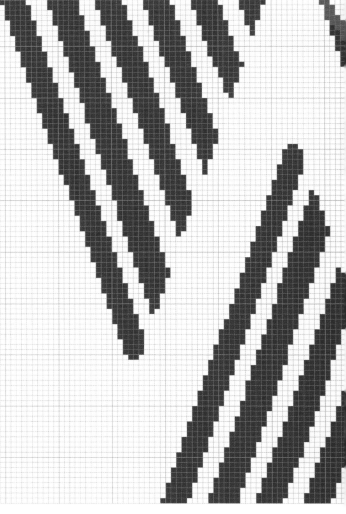

thread key

FINISHED MOTIF SIZE: 10 in (25 cm) w
X 7 in (18 cm) h

Color	Hanks	Type	Number	Name
	0.75	Appleton	992	Ivory
	1.5	Appleton	995	Red
	1.25	Appleton	483	Dark Turquoise

variations

● Refer to the chart on page 149 for yarn conversion to other tapestry yarn colors.

29 candy cane stocking

Homemade Christmas stockings are part of our family tradition. So I have created a candy cane inspired stocking to stitch, which is perfect to hang up year after year to fill with treats.

stitch stats

stitches: 112 x 143 shaped
yarn: Appleton tapestry wool
base: 7-count canvas
skill level: 2

tools and materials

- 7-count canvas, 21¾ x 21¾ in (55 x 55 cm), you can trim this later
- 4-ply Appleton Tapestry Yarn—see thread key on page 134
- Size 18 tapestry needle
- Threader (optional)
- Backing fabric, 21¾ x 21¾ in (55 x 55 cm)
- Quilted wadding, 21¾ x 21¾ in (55 x 55 cm)
- Matching sewing thread
- Pom-pom (optional)
- 12-in (30-cm) ribbon or trim for hanging
- Sewing machine to make up

method

1 Prepare your base and find the middle by folding in half and half again.

2 Check the chart on page 135 and following the yarn key on page 134, find the color shown in the middle section.

3 Thread your needle using one strand of the 4-ply tapestry yarn, following the yarn key on page 134.

4 Start stitching the first diagonal stripe—working from left to right.

5 Work through each diagonal, stitching left to right.

6 Complete the heel, toe, and top trim areas of the stocking.

variations

● Refer to the chart on page 149 for yarn conversion to other tapestry yarn colors.

finishing

1 Block/press your finished tapestry, following the directions on page 150.

2 Trim the tapestry down, leaving a ³⁄₄-in (2-cm) seam allowance around the edges.

3 Using the directions for making the template on page 152, cut out one piece of backing fabric and the two quilted wadding lining pieces.

4 Place one lining piece on top of the tapestry (right sides together) and one piece on top of the backing fabric (right sides together), then pin.

5 Sew the top edges of both pieces, then press and open out.

6 Place the right side of the linings together and the right sides of the tapestry and backing fabric together. Sew all the way around both silhouettes, leaving a gap of about 6 in (15 cm) on the back edge of the lining section.

7 Make about three snips into the tight curve of each section and across the rounded toes. Turn the stocking out and press and slip stitch the gap in the lining closed. Push the lining into the stocking.

8 Slip stitch the looped ribbon and pompom to the inside back edge and then it is ready to hang.

Note: Follow the "How to make a lined pouch" directions on page 156.

30 titan tree skirt

Tree skirts are a perfect heirloom piece and are perfect for hiding tree stands. This is a Titan project, and while the pattern is not too complex, handling a piece of canvas this size is a mammoth task.

stitch stats

stitches: 250 x 250
yarn: Appleton tapestry wool
base: 7-count canvas
skill level: 3

method

1 Prepare your base and find the middle by folding in half and half again.

2 Check the chart on page 138 and following the yarn key on page 138, find the color shown in the middle section.

3 Thread your needle with one strand of the 4-ply tapestry yarn, in the edging color, following the yarn key on page 138.

4 Count out from the middle to the inside edge of the circle (which will make the top trim of the skirt). Start to stitch left to right—working down toward the opening on the bottom right hand of the chart. Follow this edge outward to give some structure to your piece, then go back to the middle and complete the inner circle. Work outward on the skirt, a color at a time.

5 The outside edge is the hardest area to keep a tab of your stitch rows, so you may want to cross these off as you go on a copy of your chart.

tools and materials

- 7-count canvas, 3 x 3 ft (1 x 1 m)— yes it is that big!
- 4-ply Appleton Tapestry Yarn—see thread key on page 138
- Size 18 tapestry needle
- Threader (optional)
- Backing fabric, 3 x 3 ft (1 x 1 m)
- Matching sewing thread
- Sewing machine to make up

finishing

1 Block/press your finished tapestry, following the directions on page 150.

2 Trim the tapestry edges to leave a 1-in (2.5-cm) seam allowance around the edge of your work.

3 Place the pressed skirt onto the lining fabric on a flat surface (right sides together) and pin around the edges.

4 Carefully trace around the edge with tailor's chalk, then cut out the lining fabric.

5 Sew all around the edges, leaving a 8 in (20 cm) opening on one of the straight opening edges.

6 Turn the right way out, press and slip stitch the opening closed (see page 154).

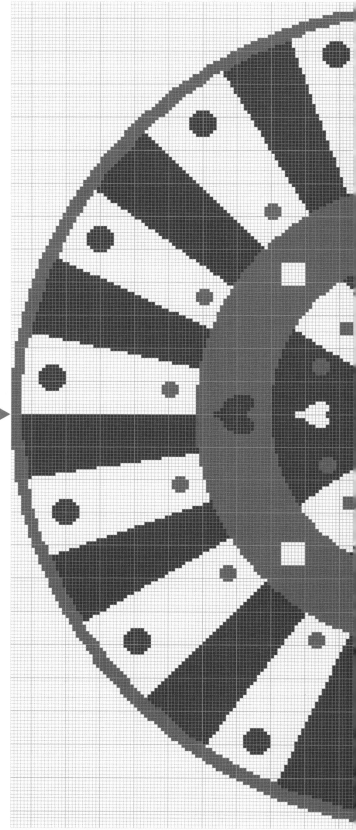

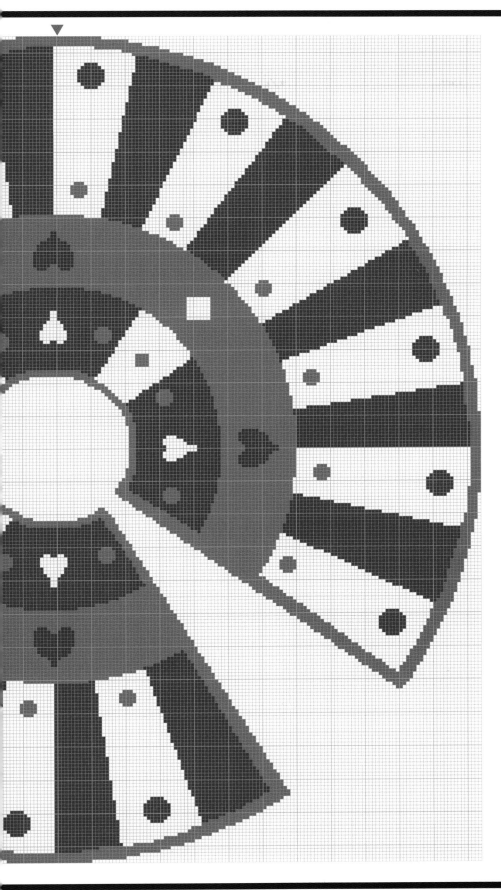

variations

● Refer to page 149 for yarn conversion to other tapestry yarn colors.

top tip

● You may want to photocopy and enlarge this chart to stitch and tick off in sections. This is ok as long as it is for personal use.

STITCHING SCHOOL

This section is about the basics—a directory of information so you can stitch with confidence … from what to keep in your stash, to stitch techniques and simple finishing methods. I have included "how-tos" on things like making your own templates and finishing off your projects with professional-looking results. There is also a list of my favorite resources. This is a chapter that you can read in depth or refer to it as you need at your leisure. By taking the time to learn a few simple stitching techniques and tricks, cross stitching will give you a lifetime's pleasure, and by using my stitches method (cross stitch + yarn + big count canvas) even beginners can get impressive results.

stitching kit

This is my guide to the key yarns and bases that you will need to make up your own stitch stash. Also, I describe the various tools and other equipment that you need. Once you have decided on your favorite base and yarn you do not have to invest a lot to start creating your own stitching kit.

canvas and bases

You can cross stitch on almost any base, I have even seen artists cross stitch on drilled lumber! But whatever the base, they all have one thing in common and that is the regular square structure of holes, which forms the grid to create your cross stitch.

The construction of standard fabric bases comes in several forms, the most common of which are **canvas, Aida,** and **evenweave.** Each of these fabrics are available in various sizes—their size is always measured by the number of holes per inch. If you put a ruler on the fabric, then count the number of holes along a row within an inch, you will get the HPI (holes per inch) or **count** of the fabric. The lower the HPI the bigger your stitches will be and vice versa. For this book I tend to work mostly in 7 and 5 count, although a couple of projects are in 11 and 14 count. The size of the base in turn determines the best yarn (and number of strands) to use.

Canvas has large open holes made from interwoven stiffened cotton. The large grid structure makes this very easy to stitch, and while 7 and 5 count (which I use regularly) is normally reserved for rug making, it is easy to stitch and get quick and impressive results. Canvas feels very stiff to start with, but the glue soon softens as you start to stitch. The other point to note is that you have to stitch every hole on a canvas design, creating a tapestry of stitches. Some find stitching the background laborious, but I think the finished results are worthwhile.

Aida is one of the more traditional cross stitch bases. It is slightly stiffened multiple rows of cotton thread interwoven (block weave) with small holes in a grid to pass the needle through. Like canvas, this is graded in HPI,

and while you can get 6 HPI (known as binca), the main sizes are 8, 11, and 14 count. The advantage of this base is that you do not have to stitch the full background, as when washed it resembles cotton fabric. You can buy linen blends and a variety of colors, but the most common are white and ivory. I prefer to use off-white.

Evenweave as the name suggests is evenly woven strands of cotton. At first glance it looks like normal fabric—you can get up to 32-count fabric (for superfine cross stitching). This is a great base to stitch on if you want to make up the item into something else—I have made napkins, tablecloths, and even clothes in this base. What I tend to do is stitch over two strands, so a 28 HPI becomes a 14 HPI.

yarn

cross stitch combinations

Base	Yarn	Strands
5 HPI canvas	4-ply tapestry	2 full yarn threads
7 HPI canvas	4-ply tapestry	1 full yarn thread
10 HPI canvas	2-ply crewel wool	2 full yarn threads
11 HPI Aida	6-strand cotton	3 strands
14 HPI Aida	6-strand cotton	2 strands
28 HPI evenweave	6-strand cotton	1 strand

Once you have decided on your base, you will need to choose your yarn. For this you can be as creative as you like, but as a rule of thumb you must have yarn which has enough coverage for the base, but is easy to stitch with. I have compiled a reference chart with the best yarn and base combinations for cross stitch (see above).

4-ply tapestry yarn by Appleton Wools is my favorite yarn for big stitching. Made famous by textile designer William Morris, these yarns have been spun and dyed in England to traditional color recipes for 150 years, using pure new British wool. Appleton's have 421 colors in their palette, all of which are available in tapestry (4 ply) and also crewel yarn (2 ply). I mainly use 15 key colors from this palette, but you can choose your own selection or stick to mine. You certainly don't have to buy all 421!

There are other companies that supply tapestry yarn (see Resources, page 158), such as Anchor and DMC, but Appleton are the only company who supply hanks of 180 ft (55 m) long. Anchor Tapisserie wool comes in 33 ft (10 m) skeins and 475 shades, and DMC skeins are 26 ft (8 m) long in 390 colors. The color equivalents are shown in the conversion chart on page 149. There are other brands too, however you will have to account for the different qualities and lengths, and I do not recommend mixing manufacturers within a project.

TIPS FOR STITCHING WOOLEN YARN

● Use the yarn in lengths of 17³⁄₄ in (45 cm), so that the yarn does not wear out as the work is stitched.
● Pull the needle vertically (not at an angle) through the canvas to reduce wear on the yarn.
● Check the yarn twist every few stitches—if the needle is turned excessively, the yarn can become too tight or unwound. When this happens hang the needle down by the thread, let it spin, and the yarn will assume its natural twist.

Stranded cotton (or floss) is made up of six strands of cotton, and it is the most common thread used in cross stitch and embroidery. It can be stitched as a whole thread or you can separate it into "strands" depending on the stitch and base used. On 14 count I use two strands, but if you want more coverage you can use three; refer to my cross stitch combinations chart opposite for a quick reference of the main bases.

There are lots of manufacturers who make floss—the large companies (DMC, Anchor, and Madeira) have hundreds of colors and even different finishes, including metallic threads. My thread of choice is DMC, as I inherited a stash of threads from my grandma, which I have continued to add to. I also use their metallics and satins in embroidery projects, and I love their new Diamante Metallics collection. I have supplied conversion charts for the key colors in my collection on page 149.

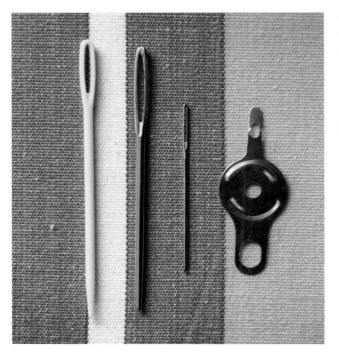

needles

For needlepoint or cross stitch, there are special tapestry needles which have a rounded "blunt" tip. This avoids damaging the fabric or stitches as you work—there is no need to "pierce" the cloth—the needle slips into spaces between threads. These needles have a longer, bigger eye to accommodate threading the larger size yarns. Like the bases, they are available in a variety of sizes.

I always use John James Needles. They have been manufacturing these needles in the UK since 1840, and I put them in all my kits. They offer needles for every occasion, including tapestry/cross stitch needles from sizes 13 to 28. The smaller the number, the fatter the needle. Size 22 is normally recommended for 14 count, and 20 for 10 count. I mainly use size 18, which can be used on crewel, tapestry, and big stitch cotton work, and is a good all rounder. For my real supersize work a size 14 is a must.

scissors and sewing stash

Apart from the base and yarn, I simply cannot do without a large yarn threader and a pair of sharp scissors. The large threaders are different from the fine wire ones used for general sewing. They have two solid ends—you choose one depending on which size yarn you are using. Place the threader through the eye of the needle, thread your yarn through its big hole, and pull back through your needle.

If you are investing in a pair of scissors there are some lovely embroidery super-sharp snipping ones available, but you can easily use a pair that you already have.

A lot of the projects in this book use a sewing machine for finishing. I have a modern Janome quilting machine, and the old family Singer, which is ancient. As we are only using a simple running stitch, you do not need an expensive machine, and if you don't have one, just use a simple handsewn backstitch to finish your work. Finally, you will need matching sewing thread for your project and a simple sharp sewing needle for any slip stitching or finishing off.

hoops and frames

Keeping the fabric under tension while stitching keeps the stitches even. For this purpose, lighter fabrics like Aida and evenweave are often stitched in a hoop, while large tapestries are often worked on floor-mounted stretcher frames.

When stitching on canvas I have never used a frame. The blocking-out process with woolen yarns is so forgiving I have not found it necessary. However, I do favor a 4-in (10-cm) hoop for working on evenweave, Aida, and any of my stranded cotton projects. With a hoop the fabric is "sandwiched" between two wooden hoops then pulled taut to create the tension, ensuring that the lines of the fabric/cross stitch are straight. Hoops are available in a variety of sizes.

trims and fabrics

I have a collection of favorite fabrics, linings, and trims which I use time and again on my projects. I have also upcycled vintage finds and old pillows. Each project gives details of the fabrics you will need to complete the project. For the pillows and larger items I always use a heavier weight cotton. For linings and simple backings try using printed cotton sheetings or simple plain fabrics, the choice is up to you. See resources on page 158 for some of my favorite sources.

starting to stitch

So you have assembled your stitching stash and chosen the first project you'd like to make—now where do you start? This section is all about preparing to stitch and brushing up on all your existing stitching techniques, so you can thread your needle with your yarn and start stitching!

preparing the base

I would recommend to cut the base fabric 4–8 in (10–20 cm) larger than the finished piece (2–4 in/ 5–10 cm around each side). It is worth taking some time to prepare the base for stitching. On Aida and evenweave make sure that you lightly steam or press out any creases from the fabric. I would advise that you take the time to either hand stitch or machine zigzag the edges to avoid any fraying of the fabric, although this is up to you.

The larger canvas pieces do not fray as readily, but the open canvas edges can snag the yarn. For this reason I usually tape the edges with duct tape, which stops both the snagging and any fraying.

Traditionally, projects are always started from the middle and worked outward. To mark the middle of your base, simply fold it in half and then in half again. You can then coordinate this with the middle of your project to start stitching. If you want an extra reference, use a ruler to mark the horizontal and vertical stitch rows which evolve from this point with a water-soluble embroidery pen. This will be covered by your stitching and easily disappears with a little water.

Frame or hoop up your base ready to get started (see **Hoops and frames**, opposite). Or if you are using canvas simply start stitching.

threading up

I recommend that you cut the yarn before threading to no longer than 17³/₄ in (45 cm) maximum. The yarn length stops longer pieces being damaged as they constantly pass through your work, but also makes life a little easier with less thread to "handle." Using your threader, thread your needle with the number of strands required for the project in the color shown on the chart.

working with charts

Each chart is a grid of colored squares. Each square represents a single stitch and the color of the square represents a different colored yarn, which is shown on the yarn key. This method is called counted cross stitch. As most projects start in the middle this is clearly shown by two large arrows on each chart highlighting the middle row. In addition, every 10th row/column is highlighted in blue on my charts to enable you to count out your squares more readily. Some people find it easier to cross off the squares as they stitch, but I have only ever done this on very complicated stitching.

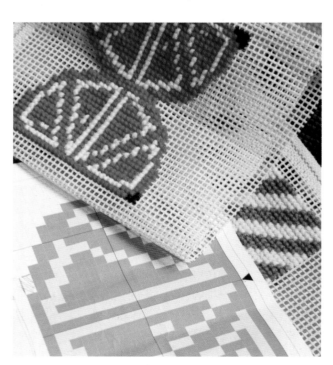

stitch methods

Now you are ready to stitch, here are the key methods that you will need to complete the projects in this book. While I have only used one stitching method (cross stitch) throughout the book there are a number of different ways to start, make, and finish your stitching.

starting off

It is important to start your stitching in the proper way (without lots of knots), otherwise your work will look "lumpy" and may even unravel. There are three main methods for starting cross stitch.

1. QUICK START

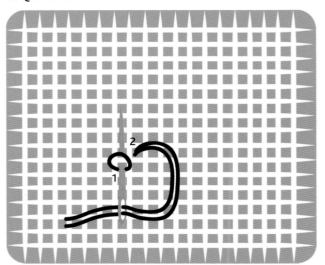

Use this method if you have an even number of strands. Cut the yarn to twice the length you need and with half the number of strands, for example, a crewel wool on 10 HPI uses two strands of yarn—cut one longer length then fold it in half to make two strands. By folding the yarn length in half a "loop" is left at the end. Thread the looped end through the needle and start to stitch from the right side. Take the needle down at point 1 then back up at point 2, pulling through but leaving a loop on the right side of the fabric. Bring the needle down at point 1 ready to make your first half cross stitch. Make sure to pass through the loop. Once the needle is through the loop, pull yarn through from the back so loop passes to the wrong side. This is your first half cross stitch. Don't pull the loop through too tightly or it will distort the stitch.

2. WASTE KNOT

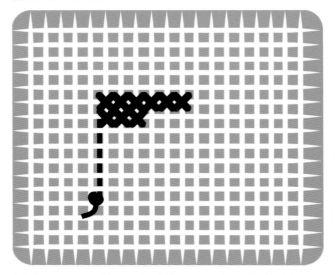

It is best to use this method if you need to stitch with an odd number of threads (eg 1 thread of yarn on a 7-count base). This is because you cannot fold the yarn in half to use the quick start method as this needs an even number of threads which can't be "doubled" (2 threads of yarn on a 5-count base, for example). Start by threading the needle with the strands of yarn specified in the project. Then make a knot at the end. About 10 holes away from where you are starting to stitch (in the direction you are going to stitch over) pass the needle from the right side through to the back and, keeping the end of the yarn against the back, start to stitch. This method "traps" the waste yarn behind the stitches you start to make, and all you need to do is snip off the knot from the right side as you approach it.

3. THREADING THROUGH/FINISHING OFF

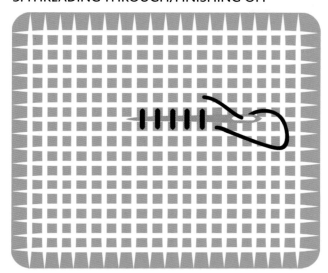

The threading through method is a "multifunction" method which is used once you have some stitches on the go. Simply run the threaded needle through the back of the last few stitches adjacent to where you are starting to stitch. This secures the thread in place ready to start stitching. You can use this method for finishing off, too. At the end of your color and/or thread, simply snip off any excess. It is also used for changing yarn in the middle of your project.

cross stitch techniques

While there is only one stitch result, there are actually two different methods for creating this stitch. My Aunty Ann prefers method one (as explained top right), while I use method two (as explained bottom right), as I like to complete each stitch as I go. It is simply a matter of personal preference. The only thing that isn't a choice is the stitch direction—every stitch must be worked in the same direction for a correct result. The larger the stitch is the more noticeable it will be if the stitches are not worked in the same direction so this discipline is essential for these big stitch projects. By this I mean that you should make sure that the second half/top of the stitch is lying in the same diagonal direction. It does not matter in which direction you choose to stitch your project, just make sure that it stays the same for the whole project. I have recommended directions in the instructions for most of the projects in this book, but the choice is yours.

METHOD 1—HALF CROSS STITCH

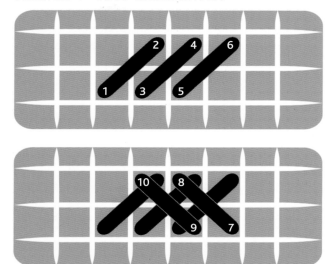

In this method you work in rows, working one half of the stitch first, then turning around and going back over the row with the top half of the cross stitch. This first half stitch is called "half cross stitch" or "tent stitch." On the illustration, the odd numbers are when the yarn is coming up from the back and the even numbers are the stitch being passed back from the front through to the back. (ie: up at 1, down at 2...) When you reach the end, simply work back over all your stitches in the opposite direction to turn the half stitch into a complete cross stitch.

METHOD 2—COMPLETE CROSS STITCH

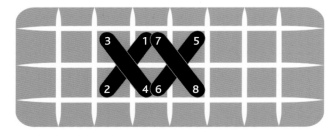

Alternatively, work the cross as you go along, up at 1, down at 2, up at 3, forming the complete stitch as you go. I hold the canvas so that the row ahead is in front of me and, as the canvas is forgivingly large, just thread the needle right to left up and down in one movement. Although this is not recommended by purists because of the "extra wear" placed on the yarn, I have not noticed a problem using tapestry or crewel yarns with this method.

DIAGONALS

If you have a row of cross stitches on the diagonal, you will need to use method 2 (see page 147). If you are working from right to left it's easier to work the stitches so that the top stitches are all lying in the same direction.

DOUBLE CROSS STITCH

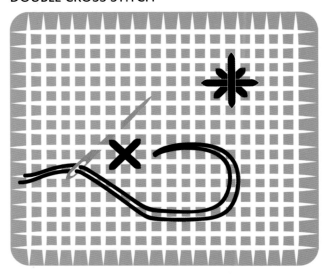

The bling worked in metallic thread on the Jewelry Roll is a stitch known as a double cross stitch, made by making a standard cross over an "X" cross. Traditionally, the stitches should be across the same number of squares—so over three or four squares in all directions—but I like to make an extra big BLING, so I have made the top square cross one square bigger.

finishing off

Finishing off is the same method as changing color, otherwise known as the threading through method (see page 147). Simply pass the thread through to the back of the fabric and thread the needle back through the last 4–5 stitches sewn, then snip off the ends.

changing color

When changing colors in the middle of a project simply change the color in the needle and use one of the starting off methods (see page 146) to start stitching in the new color. If you are stitching adjacent to other work use the threading through method (as long as the new thread isn't darker than the old one, otherwise it may "grin" through).

working through the project

Each of the projects in this book gives details of the recommended methods for stitching. I have highlighted where I think it is best to start stitching from and how to work your way through the chart until the project is complete. However, once you have mastered the various stitch techniques, it is up to you how you want to stitch. Some people prefer to do all the detail first and then fill in (my preference) and some people prefer to stitch all one color, or work in a particular direction. All I would say is just do what you feel most comfortable with.

making mistakes

It happens to all of us! Sometimes you may miscount, get distracted, or simply just mess up a few stitches. So what do you do? Fear not, it isn't the end of the world. All you need to do is to simply snip out the wrong stitches (working from the front I find is a lot easier) and then pull out the yarns. Be extremely careful not to snip the canvas or fabric—which is why I would recommend a stitch unpicker, rather than overzealous scissors—then stitch it again correctly. You can buy stitch unpickers from craft stores or online, and they are available in small and large sizes. They are sometimes called seam rippers.

my top tips

● Why not copy/enlarge the charts and tick off the squares or sections as you go, enabling you to keep track of where you are on the project?
● DIY shade card—you can create your own precut lengths in the right shades ready to stitch on the go. Simply cut a piece of card the size of a postcard and, using a hole puncher, make holes around the edge. Thread your yarn in a loop through the hole and then thread the other end through and pull—a tassel yarn organizer!
● Unpicker—invest in one. It will save you hours of snipping, should you go wrong.
● Try not to thread through the back of lighter stitches with a darker yarn, as it may "grin" through your finished project.

yarn conversion color chart

Colour	Name	Appleton	DMC	Anchor
	Ivory*	992	3823	8006
	Red*	995	321	8218
	Dark Red	505	498	8220
	Orange*	445	606	8166
	Golden Yellow*	474	934	8120
	Yellow*	553	444	8118
	Dark Grass	255	905	9156
	Grass Green*	253	907	9154
	Marine Blue*	326	9750	8794
	Dark Kingfisher	488	3847	8922
	Kingfisher*	486	3848	8920
	Dark Turquoise	483	958	8918
	Turquoise*	481	959	8916
	Purple—Bright*	456	550	8594
	Lilac*	885	210	8586
	Fuchsia	803	3804	8490
	Dark Pink*	945	956	8486
	Pink*	943	957	8482
	Brown—Chocolate*	187	898	9646
	Black*	993	310	9800
	Gray	963	169	9790

While not exact color matches, here is a list of equivalent colors from key manufacturers for all the colors used in the book. I recommend not to mix the yarn makes on the same project and also try and buy all the yarns together to make sure that they are from the same dye lot.

* The colors marked are my 15 key colors for your stitch stash.

finishing your work

Now you have finished your labor of love (as by this time you will have a relationship going with your gorgeous piece of stitching), you will want to show it off to its best advantage. Throughout the book I have suggested a way of finishing each project, but any of the pieces can be adapted and finished as you prefer. Here are some quick stitch finishing techniques.

how do I prepare for sewing?

So how do I normally finish my work? Well, I use the steam technique (see blocking, opposite) to reshape all my work quickly. I trim off any raw ends of yarn, then carefully trim the canvas down to size to suit the end use, ready to move onto the finishing process.

What do I make? My favorite finish is a big squishy pillow. I just love the endless mounds of wooly colorful pillows that adorn all our seating areas in the house, and I even have a whole window seat filled with about 20 pillows, with no room to sit. We also have walls filled with different projects framed in different styles trialed with my local framer, but sometimes I just make simple quick stitch little experiments that eventually end up as presents for my friends and family. Let me just say for the record that I am NOT a patient seamstress, which seems

daft when you consider how long you need to spend on a cross stitch. Making up the tapestry is a relaxing pastime for me, while my background in fast fashion means that any sewing (and by that I mean anything with cloth and machines involved) needs to be done in superquick time with the simplest of techniques, so if I can cut a corner, I will.

The techniques that I use to finish my work are also very quick. I can make up a pillow in less than 15 minutes. This is not down to pure skill, but a reliable technique and, of course, a steady sewing machine. The hand sewing involved is limited, if at all. There are plenty of methodologies for finishing your work, but I am going to explain those I know and love.

blocking and finishing

The process of making sure that your finished piece is square and neat is known as blocking. Fine cross stitch and needlepoint can distort the fabric during stitching, causing it to look like a parallelogram when it's complete. Blocking gets rid of this distortion.

The great thing about cross stitch in general is that the natural square shape of the work means that you do not have this issue, and a good steam iron can be your friend. The glues in the bases (which make the canvas stiff) easily soften and can be reshaped when gently warmed through. Simply steaming the reverse of a project makes it more pliable and you can ease it back into shape.

If you like, you can cut out a template of the correct square size and, after steaming, pin the corners into the square to use as a guide for ensuring that it is completely perfect. However, I have found that a little steam and reshaping helps to ease the yarn and canvas into a perfect shape without all the fuss.

framing and mounting

If you choose to have your projects framed there is nothing like the finish from a professional framer. I have used our local framer for years for all of our business. His prices are not as expensive as some bigger stores and his work is perfect. He framed all the projects in this book, and blocked and finished them too. It is worth seeking out your local framer—try to visit a few as their prices can vary. This way you are supporting a local business and also getting a top dollar finish.

If you do want to make your own frame you will need to first block out your work (see opposite), then use a cardboard cutout the same size as the finished piece to back your work, and hold it in place with a few lattice stitches running from side to side.

You can order bespoke-size frames online or simply order a mat, which is cut to size, allowing for an overlap of ¼ in (5 mm) over your work on each side. Secure your blocked work in your chosen frame or mat, following the manufacturer's directions.

looking after your work

You will have invested many hours on your finished project, so it's important to take a little time to learn how to look after your work. I have collected and treasured many homespun stitching projects, and I always wonder if the ladies (or gents) knew at the time of stitching that it would eventually end up in my home. However small your handstitched piece, it is an heirloom!

As most of the items in the book are made from 100 percent virgin wool they are prone to moths. This doesn't mean that you need to hide them away with moth balls— in fact, it is better to keep them out on display and properly aired. Make sure that the item is not in direct sunlight as the work will fade over time if it's kept in strong light. If your project gets a little grubby, I wouldn't recommend putting it in the washing machine, as the yarn may shrink

and the canvas disintegrate. Instead, gently vacuum any dust and use a damp cloth to remove any stains.

finishing flourishes

Well, as you may have gathered by now, I am a haberdashery fiend. If it's big, fluffy, or colorful then I grab it like a magpie and put it in my stash. I discovered the oversized rick rack trim that I use in a lot of my projects on a vacation in France, and the company that made it still supplies us with our stock today. It comes in a variety of sizes and colors and adds a retro panache to the projects.

Supersized rick rack has the same effect on me as does any ribbon, bobble, or bell. I am a self-confessed pom-pom addict, and since discovering the "quick pom-pom maker tool" my children and I whip them up in minutes, and they look great sewn on the corners of any pillow. I have kept the finishing techniques simple throughout the book, but if you want to add some trim there is a quick tutorial with the pillow directions on page 156.

making templates

I have used plenty of templates supplied at the back of cross-stitch craft books, but they are hard to photocopy accurately and the stitching can distort during making up. Templates are great if you are making something entirely from fabric or paper to size, but with big cross stitch it's better to make your own. If you are feeling brave, mark out straight onto the fabric.

what is a template?

A template is basically a pattern, usually made from paper. They are the "blocks" used for cutting out the pieces of your project ready for stitching, as well as acting as a guide for placement of the finishing touches. Some designers include a seam allowance in their templates and some do not (you have to add this yourself around the outside). The lack of standards on this is another reason why I prefer to make my own.

You can use any kind of paper to make your templates, but as some of my projects are quite large, I usually use brown kraft paper. It is cheap and available in reams, and big. You can use it for lots of other things like wrapping gifts and crafting, so it's a great thing to have in your stash.

You will need:
- Kraft paper (available in sheets, reams, or rolls)
- Weights or pins (heavy books will suffice)
- Soft pencil
- Large ruler or right angle
- Scissors (for cutting paper)

how to make your own templates/paper patterns

There are a few simple steps to making your own template for your stitching project, but first of all you need to prepare your project as described in the blocking section on page 150. Here is a step-by-step guide:
- Block out your work and press.
- Trim any excess or loose yarns to avoid "tangling" when stitching up.
- Carefully trim the tapestry edges to leave a seam allowance around the outside. I usually leave 1 in (2.5 cm) around every edge (or less on smaller projects).
Tip: You can use the grid of the canvas as a guide, for example, on a 7-count fabric 7 holes = 1 in (2.5 cm), so allow 7 holes all the way around your finished piece. You are now left with a finished shape which includes your tapestry and a 1-in (2.5-cm) seam allowance all the way around the edge.
- Press your kraft paper lightly (no steam) to make sure that it is flat.
- Place your trimmed piece onto your paper on a large

flat work surface. Weight it down or pin it in place and carefully trace around the edge with a pencil, drawing your shape onto the paper.

● When the tapestry is removed there will be an outline on your paper. Double check that there are no "bumpy bits"—smoothing out the pattern lines or using a ruler for straight edges.

● Carefully cut around the outline. You now have a basic shaped template which perfectly matches your tapestry, including seam allowance.

● Lay the template over your tapestry to double check the shape and fit.

1. SQUARE/RECTANGLE TEMPLATES
If you are making a basic stuffed pillow (no envelope back) you can use the template method as above to create your square. Alternatively, you can measure the sides and draw your square/rectangle using a right angle ruler directly onto the paper and then double check your tapestry against it before cutting out the paper template.

This is also a good method for double checking your blocking. If the tapestry is a little skewed you can use this perfect right-angled template to pin out your work and steam.

2. ENVELOPE PILLOW TEMPLATES
If you would like to create an envelope back from your square template, you will need to mark out the square as above, then add 4 in (10 cm) to the two opposite sides you want to overlap. For example, if your square is 16 in (40 cm) wide you will need to add 8 in (20 cm), making one edge now 23¾ in (60 cm) long. Mark the middle point and draw a line (in the example it would be at the 12 in/30 cm point), then cut out these two pieces of paper. They should be exactly the same size.
Note: It is always a good idea to lay the cut pieces onto your tapestry to double check that the overlap works before you use them to cut out your backing fabric.

3. SHAPED TEMPLATES
Shaped templates follow the same methodology explained in the template steps above. Examples of the shaped templates would be the Sleep Tight Mask or the Russian Doll Pillow. Just take a little extra care drawing around your work, especially the curves, and put the paper pattern on top of your tapestry afterward to double check that you have drawn it correctly.

4. LININGS
You do not need to create multiple new templates for the linings, as they follow the same pattern as the backing fabrics. Once you have made one template you can use this to cut out your multiple layers.

It is worth taking a little extra care while making the templates, as accurate patterns will save you lots of time when stitching.

5. BADGES, AIDA, AND EVENWEAVE PROJECTS
The projects that use templates in this book don't have a set tapestry edge, so I have described how big to make your template ready for finishing in the finishing section of each project. For the round mustache badge I have made a template to size (see below).

ready-done templates
I have included a template of the mustache badge (see page 72) as this is not something that you can readily make—simply photocopy the template and cut out.

MUSTACHE TEMPLATE

get set, stitch!

Now you are nearly there! You have your project and template and you are ready to finish stitching it up. This section is a step-by-step reference of all your stitching needs to complete your project, including how to finish your work by hand, how to do the different stitches, and how to add the final flourishes, such as pom-poms and trims.

making up requirements

All of the projects use a sewing machine for making up, but if you do not have one you can stitch up using simple backstitch—it will just take you a little longer. You will also need to learn how to slip stitch to close your openings once your project is "turned out."

You will need:
- Sewing machine
- Matching thread for your project
- Sharp general needle
- Scissors
- Iron for pressing

stitching details
BACKSTITCH

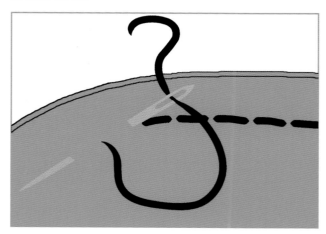

You can use this versatile stitch if you don't have a sewing machine, but it is also a good basic embroidery stitch, often used in top stitching. It involves taking the needle backward and then down through the fabric and back up again a stitch ahead—you are overstitching yourself,

which makes this such a good "lock stitch." However, I would recommend that you beg, borrow, or book a slot at your local stitch studio for a sewing machine instead, as it will be much quicker to complete the big projects.

SLIP STITCH

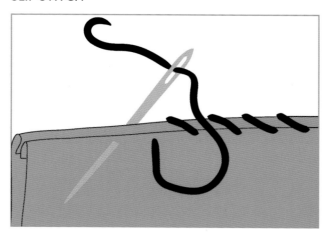

This handy stitch is used for invisibly closing gaps in your stitching. Used on projects like the Russian Doll Pillow (see page 34), it is worked with the project the right way out. Make sure that the seam allowance on each side is placed inside and hold the two edges together (you can pin them together if you have a large opening). Pass the needle through both sides of the fold, working right to left, which, if you keep your stitching on the edge, will leave an almost invisible finish.

basic machine stitching

Joining your tapestry to the cloth is the same process as sewing two pieces of fabric together on a machine.
- Place the two right sides together, and align the edges that need to be stitched.

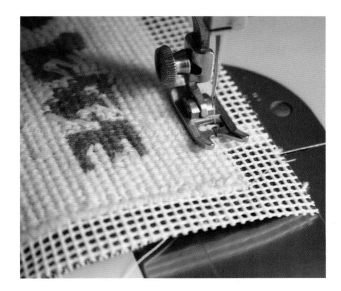

- Pin in place if required.
- Place on the machine with the tapestry side up.
- Follow the edge of your tapestry (slightly over the first stitch) as the seam allowance. This way you will not have any "grinning" of the canvas when it's the right way around.
- Reinforce each end with a few extra stitches to make sure that it doesn't unravel.

turning a corner

- Sew along the first side as above.
- Finish at the corner with the needle "down" in the fabric, then lift the presser foot up.
- Turn your work around so that you are ready to stitch the next side, and put the presser foot back down.
- Continue to stitch.
- Before turning the project the right way around, trim excess fabric around the corner so that it does not bulk out the finished look.
- Turn the project the right way around and push out the corner with the blunt end of a knitting needle.
- Press on the fabric side.

curved edges

- Curves are the same as stitching a straight edge. Make sure that you prepare the edges after stitching, which allows the fabric to move and lie flat when turned out.
- When stitching follow the line of the tapestry, sewing slowly as you go.

- Before turning out your work, snip out little "V" shapes into the seam allowance, then turn out, and press.
- This method needs to be used on the turns of the stockings and nose area of the Sleep Tight Mask, as well as for shaped pillows like the Heart Swirls and Russian Doll.

making up methods

SIMPLE STUFFED PILLOW

Use this method for: All of the shaped pillows. If you don't want to make an envelope back, then follow these instructions to make up any of the pillows with a simple stuffing and no envelope back:

- Block your work and make your template.
- Cut out your backing fabric using your template.
- Place over the front of your tapestry right sides together, and pin.
- Machine stitch along the edges, turning the corners, and leaving a 6-in (15-cm) opening on one side. Turn the right way around and push out the corners. Press on the fabric side.
- Stuff your pillow with a suitable filler.
- Slip stitch your opening closed.

ENVELOPE PILLOW

Use this method for: Any of the square pillows you would like to make with an envelope back.

- Block your work and make your templates.
- Cut out your two pieces of backing fabric using your templates.

● Turn over a ½-in (1-cm) double fold hem on the two edges you want to overlap, press, and top stitch the edge to keep in place.

● Place the first piece of fabric over the tapestry right sides together, then place the other piece on top, making sure that the hemmed edges are overlapping and in the middle with the right side down. Pin in place.

● Machine stitch around all the edges, trim the corners, and turn the right way around.

● You now have an envelope pillow ready to take a filler. I tend to opt for one size up so that my pillow is plump.

ADDING TRIMMINGS

Use this method for: Adding welt, bobble trim, or rickrack to any of your pillows.

● Block your work and make your templates.

● Cut your trim to size. If you are making an envelope pillow, only add bobble trim on the non-cross-over sides (as the bobble is very bulky to sew).

● Place your trim over the right side of the tapestry, with the bobbles facing into the middle of the tapestry, ensuring that the anchoring tape for the bobbles isn't intruding on the stitching, otherwise it will show. Baste the trim in place.

● Place the backing fabric over the trim, right sides together, and stitch up as above. **Tip:** Change the machine foot to a zipper foot so you can get up to the edge.

● Finish as before.

SIMPLE LININGS

Use this method for: Bling Bling Jewel Wrap, Sleep Tight Mask, Noel Bunting, and Titan Tree Skirt.

The process of lining an item like the Bling Bling Jewel Wrap is effectively the same as making a simple pillow. Trim, make, and cut out the templates and stitch up as before. Turn the right way out and slip stitch closed, then press. If you are adding loops, they are added at the same stage as the trimming (see left), basting into place before placing on your backing fabric.

SIMPLE LINED POUCH

Use this method for: Groovy Granny EyeGlass Case, Retro Phone Case, and Mix Tape Tablet Cover.

The lined pouch just adds in one more process into your stitching.

● Block your work and make your template.

● Cut 1 x backing fabric and 2 x lining fabrics from your template.

● Place one piece of lining onto your tapestry and one piece of lining onto your backing fabric, right sides together, then turn under and pin the edge that will be your 'opening' on each of these pieces.

● Sew this opening edge on both of the pieces. Press flat.

● Place the right sides of each of these pieces together, lining against lining and tapestry against the backing fabric. Make sure that the seamed ends are aligned.

● Starting in the lining section, sew around the edge of your work as above, finish, leaving an opening large enough to turn out your work.

● Turn out, prepare and push out corners. Slip lining inside tapestry pouch; slipsitch in place at inside top edge.

LINED PADDED POUCH

Use this method for: Rainbow Cozy and Candy Cane Stocking. This method is made up exactly the same as above with the addition of a couple of processes:

● Block your work and make your template.

● Cut 1 x backing fabric, 2 x lining fabrics, 2 x wadding from your template.

● Place one piece of wadding onto the wrong side of your tapestry and one piece of wadding onto the wrong side of your backing fabric. Baste around the edges.

● Follow the process above for a simple lined pouch, but

can make them in no time at all. I use the extra-large pom-pom maker, available from plenty of stitch stores (including mine). I use excess tapestry yarn or odd balls of yarn from other crafts to make up matching pom-poms. Follow the manufacturer's instructions and when "tying off" leave a long end (about 12 in/30 cm) and thread both these long ends into the needle. Stitch these ends into your stocking or on top of a teacozy, securing into place.

before turning out cut back the wadding to the edge of the stitching so that it will not add too much bulk when turned out.

LINED ZIPPERED POUCH

Use this method for: Crayon Pencil Case, Lipstick Makeup Purse, and Orange Segment Purse.

● Block your work and make your template.
● Cut 1 x backing fabric and 2 x lining fabrics from your template.
● Place one edge of your zipper onto your tapestry and one onto the opening edge of your backing fabric. Baste and using a zipper foot, stitch into place.
● Fold back on itself so the right sides of the tapestry and backing fabric are together, and sew around the edges. You now have a zippered pouch that opens.
● Put the two lining pieces right sides together and stitch around the bottom and side edges, turn out, and press.
● Place the lining inside your zippered pouch, with the wrong side facing the wrong side of the tapestry. Fold in the top seam allowance and pin/baste it to the exposed seam of the zipper inside to hide this seam.
● Slip stitch into place.

POM-POMS

Use this method for: Rainbow Cozy and Candy Cane Stocking. I love a big wooly pom-pom and since discovering the quick pom-pom makers I have found that I

POUFFE

Use this method for: Groovy Pouffe.

● Block your work and make your templates. The base circle is easy. To make the side measure around the edge of your circle, draw this plus 2 in (5 cm) as a long side onto your template paper. Measure 12 in (30 cm) for the other edge and you have a super-long rectangle.
● Cut out the side fabric from the long rectangle and a circle for the base.
● Pin the edge of the long rectangle around the edge of the tapestry circle right sides together and stitch, leaving the seam allowance of 1 in (2.5 cm) for the side opening pinched together at the end.
● Pin and stitch the base in the same way. Snip the curved edges, then turn out and press.
● Stuff the pouffe with plenty of old linen, towels, and fabric scraps. It needs to be super-full to work as a seat.
● Pin and slip stitch the side opening shut.

CLUTCH

Use this method for: Big Bow Clutch.

● Block your work and make your template.
● Cut 2 x backing fabrics from your template.
● Fold one of the backing fabric pieces in half, wrong sides together (as if it was the same size as the clutch), this will make the front of your inner pouch.
● Trim 1/2 in (1 cm) off the edge at the bottom. Place this piece onto the bottom of the other backing fabric, right sides together and baste.
● Place the backing piece and bow tapestry right sides together, with the bow at the opposite end to the pouch.
● Sew around the edge, starting at the pouch end, leaving an opening of about 4 in (10 cm).
● Trim, turn the right way out, then slip stitch the opening closed.

resources

While not exhaustive, this is a list of some of my favorite stitching suppliers and resources. The websites will give you further information and contact details in your area.

Arts Crafts USA
Online craft store for everything that you need for cross stitch and other crafts
www.artscraftsusa.com

Cloth Kits
A 70's crafty company revived by local friend Kay
Clothkits Ltd, 1-2 St Pancras, Chichester, West Sussex PO19 7SJ, United Kingdom
01243 533180
www.clothkits.co.uk

Clover
Suppliers of pom-pom makers, pins, needles, and scissors
www.clover-usa.com

Coats & Clark
US yarns and great stitching reference
www.coatsandclark.com

Cross Stitcher & Needlework Magazine
US modern magazine dedicated to cross stitch and needlework
www.c-sn.com

Cross Stitchers
Everything that you will need for cross stitch
www.crossstitchers.com

Design-a-Cushion
Pillows in all shapes and sizes and deliver worldwide
www.design-a-cushions.co.uk

DMC
French yarns and stitching bits with worldwide distributors
www.dmc.com

eBay
Bargain job lot fabrics and yarns
www.eBay.com

Etsy
Home to many crafters, for fabric and stitching inspiration
www.etsy.com

Home-Sew Inc
Sells everything that you will need for sewing and crafts including ribbons, trims fabrics, sewing machine and supplies
www.homesew.com

Jacqui P
Home of my kits, charts, fabrics, and supplies.
PO Box 134, Arundel, West Sussex BN18 8BU, United Kingdom
info@jacquip.com
www.jacquip.com

Janome
Sewing machines of all levels
www.janome.com

John James Needles
Needles galore
www.jjneedles.com

Pearl and Earl
Home of my home and celebration collection
PO Box 134, Arundel, West Sussex BN18 8BU, United Kingdom
info@pearlandearl.com
www.pearlandearl.com

The Silver Needle
Events and cross stitch classes
www.thesilverneedle.co/crossstitchclassesandweekends.html

Traveling Tours
Events and retreats
travelingtogether.net/Traveling/default.cfm

Zweigart
My favored cross stitch canvas and bases
www.zweigart.com

index

acknowledgments

Jacqui would like to thank the following people...

My family, The Horton Clan, for just about everything—my mom and dad for their never-ending support, Aunty Ann my stitching queen, and Uncle Stuart for not minding being a stitching widower. Leeann for letting me use her kitchen table and plying me with banana cake and giggles at the end. Kati for being my crafty guinea pig, and Libby for being the best creative assistant a mom could ask for. Thank you to grandma Dora for her colorful life and inspiration—I hope she is watching from above with approval.

Cara at DMC and all at Janome for supplying me with machines and stitching goodies, Appleton, John James, and Heritage Stitches for providing the materials for my craft, and to the team at Cross Stitcher for giving me a crafty voice.

Special thanks to Judith, Janis, Alice, Russell, and Stewart, Fil Rouge, and the creative crew who made my designs come to life.

With the biggest thanks of all to all of my customers past, present, and future, who have given me the opportunity to spend my work life creating things that I love, and without whom I would not have been able to write this book.

Fil Rouge would like to thank the following people...
Janis Utton, Kathy Steer, Alice King, and Russell Sadur.